The Prophetic Theology of George Tyrrell

AMERICAN ACADEMY OF RELIGION

Studies in Religion

Thomas J. J. Altizer, Editor
James O. Duke, Associate Editor

Number 22
The Prophetic Theology of George Tyrrell
by David F. Wells
James O. Duke, Editor

The Prophetic Theology
of
George Tyrrell

by
David F. Wells

Scholars Press

Distributed by
SCHOLARS PRESS
101 Salem Street
PO Box 2268
Chico, CA 95927

The Prophetic Theology of George Tyrrell

by
David F. Wells

Library of Congress Cataloging in Publication Data
Wells, David F.
  The prophetic theology of George Tyrrell.

  (American Academy of Religion studies in Religion; no. 22
ISSN 0084-6287)
  Bibliography: p.
  1. Tyrrell, George, 1861-1909.   I. Title. II. Series: American
Academy of Religion.   AAR studies in religion; no. 22.
BX4705.T9W44   230'.2'0924   79-27097
ISBN 0-89130-376-6 pbk.

Printed in the United States of America
1   2   3   4   5   6
Edwards Brothers, Inc.
Ann Arbor, Michigan 48104

To my teachers

sine qua non

TABLE OF CONTENTS

ACKNOWLEDGMENTS

This book began to germinate in my mind about ten years ago. That process might have come to naught but for the kindly encouragement of Professor H. Cunliffe-Jones of the University of Manchester, England, to whom I wish to pay special tribute. Since then there have been others, too numerous to mention by name, who have either heartened me by their agreements or provoked me by their disagreements; to these, too, I give my thanks.

Portions of an essay on Tyrrell that first appeared in *The Harvard Theological Review* (copyright 1972 by the President and Fellows of Harvard College) are used with permission in this book. I wish to thank those who have allowed me to work with unpublished materials and to use quotations and excerpts from these in the pages which follow. They are Mrs. Katherine Pirenne, Sister Teresa, the Librarian of St. Andrew's University, the Reverend Francis Edwards, S.J., and the Librarian of Blackfriars, Oxford.

LIST OF ABBREVIATIONS

1. MANUSCRIPTS

Archives, Eng. Prov. S.J. — Provincial Archives of the English Society
of Jesus, Farm Street, London

Bod. Lib. — Bodleian Library, Oxford University,
England

Br. Mus. — Department of Manuscripts, British
Museum, London

St. And. Lib. — St. Andrew's University Library, Edinburgh,
Scotland

2. TYRRELL'S WORKS

A&L I *Autobiography and Life of George Tyrrell*. Vol. 1:
Autobiography of George Tyrrell, 1861-1884. Edited and
arranged by M.D. Petre. London: Edward Arnold, 1912.

A&L II *Autobiography and Life of George Tyrrell*. Vol. 2: *Life of George
Tyrrell, 1884-1909*. By M.D. Petre. London: Edward Arnold,
1912.

CCR *Christianity at the Crossroads*. London, New York, Bombay, and
Calcutta: Longmans, Green and Co., 1909.

CF *The Church and the Future*. Edinburgh: Turnbull and Spears,
1903.

EF *Essays on Faith and Immortality*. Arranged and edited by M.D.
Petre. London: Edward Arnold, 1914.

ER *External Religion: Its Use and Abuse*. London, New York, and
Bombay: Longmans, Green and Co., 1901.

FMI *The Faith of the Millions: A Selection of Past Essays*. First
Series. London, New York, and Bombay: Longmans, Green and
Co., 1901.

GTL *George Tyrrell's Letters*.

HS *Hard Sayings: A Selection of Meditations and Studies*. London,
New York, and Bombay: Longmans, Green and Co., 1904.

LC *Lex Credendi: A Sequel to Lex Orandi*. London, New York,
Bombay and Calcutta: Longmans, Green and Co., 1906.

LO *Lex Orandi, or Prayer and Creed*. London, New York, Bombay,
and Calcutta: Longmans, Green and Co., 1903.

M   *Medievalism: A Reply to Cardinal Mercier.* London, New York, Bombay, and Calcutta: Longmans, Green and Co., 1908.

MAL   *A Much Abused Letter.* London, New York, Bombay, and Calcutta: Longmans, Green and Co., 1906.

OW   *Oil and Wine.* London, New York, Bombay, and Calcutta: Longmans, Green and Co., 1907.

RF   *Religion as a Factor of Life.* Exeter: William Pollard and Co., 1902.

T&C   *Through Scylla and Charybdis or the Old Theology and the New.* London, New York, Bombay, and Calcutta: Longmans, Green and Co., 1907.

3. COUNCIL DOCUMENTS

Con. DV — Dogmatic Constitution on Divine Revelation (*Dei Verbum*)

Con. GS — Pastoral Constitution on the Church in the Modern World (*Gaudium et Spes*)

Con. LG — Constitution on the Church (*Lumen Gentium*)

Con. SC — Constitution on the Liturgy (*Sacrosanctum Concilium*)

Dec. AA — Decree on the Apostolate of the Laity (*Apostolicam Actuositatem*)

Dec. AG — Decree on the Church's Missionary Activity (*Ad Gentes*)

Dec. CD — Decree on the Bishop's Pastoral Office in the Church (*Christum Dominus*)

Dec. OE — Decree on the Eastern Catholic Churches (*Orientalium Ecclesiarum*)

Dec. IM — Decree on the Instruments of Social Communication (*Inter Mirifica*)

Dec. PC — Decree on the Appropriate Renewal of the Religious Life (*Perfectae Caritatis*)

Dec. PO — Decree on Ministry and Life of Priests (*Presbyterorum Ordinis*)

Dec. UR — Decree on Ecumenism (*Unitatis Redintegratio*)

Decln. NA — Declaration on the Relationship of the Church to Non-Christian Religions (*Nostra Aetate*)

Decln. DH — Declaration on Religious Freedom (*Dignitatis Humanae*)

INTRODUCTION

The Catholic world of 1870 was vastly different from that of 1970. The 1870s belonged to Veuillot, Franzelin, Pio Nono, to political absolutism and high orthodoxy. The 1970s have been stamped with the benign image of Pope John XXIII and Cardinal Bea. These are the years of unprecedented theological liberty when Rahner, Küng, and Suenens have forced a new flexibility, a new fluidity, into the structure and functioning of the Church. A century ago the Church was isolated and embattled. It was launching a fierce counter attack against that triumvirate of evils, liberalism, modern civilization, and progress. Today, it is seeking accommodation not only to political and secular power but also to some of those religious notions which once seemed so menacing. These two worlds are represented by the two Vatican Councils, the first being held in 1870 and the second from 1962 to 1965. And lying between them are the stepping stones from the one age to the other; it is one of these transitional moments that is the focus of this study.

The first group of stepping stones was so dangerous, so deceptive, that one wonders how the transition was even begun. It was constituted by a series of political and theological controversies whose direct interconnections may seem obscure but of whose close relation there can be little doubt. These debates were sparked when attempts were made at adjusting Catholic faith to the intellectual and political realities of the modern world. Out of these discussions emerged Liberal Catholicism, Americanism, the Sillon, Action Française, and Modernism.

Each movement had to be condemned by the Church. And yet, in spite of their ignominious end, they did lead to a development in the Catholic mind. Looking back on them from the vantage point of Vatican II, they seem less menacing, less *avant garde*, than they did then. But this is because they are viewed from within the atmosphere and achievements of the new age to which they were pointers.

The Second Vatican Council, of course, had no intention of reversing the warnings and condemnations which had terminated these movements. It did not even address itself to these matters. On the other hand, by accepting a plurality of theologies under the rubric of orthodoxy, the Council did endorse some ideas upon which the Church had formerly frowned. It is the newer emphases, the different cast in which Catholic thought is being placed, the innovative principles by which it is now being framed, that is throwing a far softer light on these earlier struggles. Inadvertently, therefore, the Council has opened the door to a new understanding of these transitional crises; they, too, must be allowed to enjoy the benefits of *aggiornamento*.

It is not uncommon for each of these movements to be treated in isolation from the others. The many studies on Modernism, for example, have usually followed this procedure, thereby abstracting it from the broad flow of ecclesiastical and secular events. When this is done, it is easier to accept the view, which is set out in the encyclical *Pascendi*, that Modernism was really a cunningly contrived plot the chief goal of which was the overthrow of the Church.[1] A serious attempt at eliciting the real significance of the movement for today, however, must reject these shortcuts. For Modernism was symptomatic of the profound difficulties which the whole Church faced. It was the child of a marriage, perhaps illegal but many felt inevitable, between Catholic faith and contemporary culture. It was more of an historical and cultural necessity than a fifth column. The confluence of revolutionary forces in the Church forced together thinkers of uneven abilities, different temperaments, diverse interests, and even competing theologies. They came to constitute a loose-knit "school," but what bound them together was sometimes little more than the innocence of shared comradery and only occasionally the desire to hatch subversive plots. To be sure, there was a measure of intellectual coherence and tactical agreement between them, and, furthermore, some of the Modernists did speak of destroying the Church. Their weapons were those of the mind, however; if they gave the appearance of fostering secret intrigues, it must be remembered that they did not enjoy even a token of that liberty which Catholic theologians now deem indispensable to their proper functioning in the Church. Certainly there is not a shred of evidence that the Modernists ever established a clandestine organization to achieve by stealth what they had failed to win by argument.[2] In evaluating Modernism, then, the current of events that leads up to 1870 and flows on into the present must ever be kept in view if distortion and misrepresentation are to be avoided.

The second line of stepping stones which leads from the one age into the other passes through the "Nouvelle Théologie" of the 1940s. It seems that no scholar has ever admitted to being part of this movement (was it even a movement?), and so it is difficult to give a precise account of what actually constituted the novelty of this theology. It would probably be more accurate to speak of a new spirit than a new theology. It is certainly interesting to note that during the 1940s those conservatives who felt discomforted by these developments and began to speak of a fresh outbreak of Modernism in the Church were surprisingly vague as to where deviations from the faith were actually taking place.[3] If there was a recrudescence of Modernism amongst the new thinkers—Bouillard,

Daniélou, Congar, von Balthazar, Rahner—one has to say that it was a more tactful, more ecclesiastically responsible, and more orthodox form of it. The new approach was felt principally in biblical and historical studies. In 1943, Pius XII broke new ground, for official teaching, with his encyclical *Divino Afflante Spiritu*. He opened up biblical studies to moderate form criticism. This decision undoubtedly emerged from the discussions in the early 1940s. On the historical side a corresponding relaxation of the older approach can also be detected. Bouillard's study, *Conversion et grâce chez Thomas d'Aquin* (1941), is a case in point. In this book, he argued that the Church is not irrevocably committed to the use of Aristotelian categories. By confusing "essence" with "historicity," the Church had absolutized what was relative, thereby giving the status of truth to that which was merely passing philosophical fashion. Human thought is always tinged by relativity; even Thomas's thought ought to be seen in this way.

In 1950, *Humani generis* was issued as a corrective to these ideas, but it is a far cry from the encyclical *Pascendi* by which Modernism was ended. The encyclical does not deny the element of relativity in human thought; rather, it admits that the unchanging core of faith must be presented in theological wrappings which are not antiquated. On the other hand, there is an insistence that faith in its essence is immutable. In short, the encyclical steers a middle course between left-wing Modernism—Tyrrell is an exception at this point—and the kind of scholarship associated with nineteenth century neoscholasticism. The possibility of making this kind of distinction between that which is absolute and that which is relative had been urged upon the Church by Tyrrell, von Hügel, and others and, in time, it was to become the linchpin around which the theology of Vatican II turns. Thus the problems precipitated by the "Nouvelle Théologie" opened the way for a more flexible handling of theological issues, and so speeded the transition into a new Catholic age.

It would seem clear, then, that Vatican II was not so much a beginning as an end; it was to a large extent an official and legal summary of those ideas which had been bandied about in the 1940s and 1950s and which were considered fruitful. It marks the point of forward progress in theological endeavor during this time. But it also provides a fascinating vantage point from which Modernism can now be re-examined.

In Europe, the task of re-evaluation has been undertaken energetically and with considerable sophistication. A recent though inadequate study on Loisy,[4] for example, has been produced; bibliographies prepared;[5] unpublished letters are being released;[6] and a number of impressive studies, either on aspects of Modernist belief or on specific Modernists, have appeared.[7]

The English Modernists are beginning to receive attention, too, but with the important exception of George Tyrrell.[8] As late as 1962, Emile Poulat observed that no bibliography of Tyrrell's writings had even been published, though there were at this time several doctoral dissertations available which had attempted to make such a list. It was not until 1969 that Loome published the first Tyrrell bibliography, citing his published writings but omitting the voluminous private correspondence which is still largely unpublished.[9] To date, only two collections of his letters have appeared, and the first was somewhat marred by the editorial work done on it.[10]

When one turns from bibliography to analysis, the neglect of Tyrrell's theology is just as evident. Recently there have appeared a number of journal articles dealing with aspects of his thought. But one looks in vain for a fullscale attempt to grasp the whole range of his thought. John Ratté devoted only a third of his book to Tyrrell,[11] and Meriol Trevor gave him only a chapter.[12] Before this, Alfred Loisy divided a book between Tyrrell and Bremond.[13] But, for a complete analysis, and one which does not deal with Tyrrell's thought in conjunction with other matters, one has to go back to Johannes Stam's George Tyrrell, published in 1938, or to Lewis May's Father Tyrrell and the Modernist Movement, published in 1932. Before this time the only studies which were published on Tyrrell himself, apart from general studies on Modernism, were those of Maude Petre[14] and of Raoul Gout (L'affaire Tyrrell: Un épisode de la crise Catholique [1909]).

In the absence of any fresh analyses of Tyrrell, those interested in Tyrrell's theology are forced to use the older studies on Modernism. In fact, some of these studies are still vital to the study of the leaders in the movement. In certain respects they are not dated at all. Michele Ranchetti's The Catholic Modernists, published in 1969, has not added very much to the two magisterial studies which appeared in 1934 and 1929, respectively, Alec Vidler's The Modernist Movement in the Roman Church and Jean Rivière's Le modernisme dans l'église. But, in another respect, the earlier studies and perhaps even Ranchetti's are seriously dated because of Vatican II. Indeed, it is the paucity of contemporary interpretation which accounts for the republication of A. L. Lilley's Modernism in 1970. With the new edition of Tyrrell's works now being offered comes a new obligation to interpret him afresh vis-à-vis the changed situation in the Church. That this has not been undertaken to date is something of an enigma.

In the pages which follow, I have tried to develop an understanding of the theology of George Tyrrell that is historically sensitive but re-evaluated from a post-Vatican II position. I am conscious of the potential for controversy which such a study contains, for it seems to imply that yesterday's heresy has become today's orthodoxy. If this is the case, conservative Catholics at least will be discomforted, for no notion of doctrinal development can account for a capitulation of this magnitude given the brief period of time which is involved. Consequently, it needs to be said at the outset that my concern centers wholly on Tyrrell; where questions of relationship between his thought and contemporary views arise, my sole intention remains that of eliciting the proper significance of the Irish priest's ideas.

When the Church closed the door on Modernism, it could not close the door on the central problem with which the Modernists were struggling—the relation between Christ and culture, the sacred and the profane. This is an issue to be reworked by every generation. It is once again being examined by the Church today, and the struggle of the Modernist period may have some interesting lessons to teach the Church. If so, Tyrrell's theology will become far more significant than Pius X ever feared to dream.

Chapter One

A MODERN MOVEMENT

Between the years 1890 and 1907, the Roman Catholic Church passed through a period of internal friction more painful than anything which had happened since the time of the Reformation. It was the climax to a mutually felt antipathy that had developed between the Catholic hierarchy on the one hand and on the other those proponents of reform who came to be known as Modernists. In 1907, the Movement was, as it were, gored to death by two papal bulls, the first of which was *Lamentabili sane exitu,* and the second, *Pascendi dominici gregis.*[1] Disciplinary action was implemented throughout the Church, some of the leaders of the movement already having been excommunicated; in 1910, the Oath against Modernism was instituted in an effort to safeguard the Church's future purity. These measures, by any reckoning Draconian, successfully eliminated the ideas for which the Modernist reformers had agitated, and they returned the Church to the orthodoxy of the late nineteenth century as defined by the Pope.

Michele Ranchetti has traced the origins of the movement, such as it was, back to the year 1864. It should be observed, however, that it was not until the closing decade of the nineteenth century that Modernist influence was really felt in the Church. In France, for example, Loisy lost his position at the Institut Catholique in 1893, partly for venturing outside the parameters of what was considered to be orthodox and partly for angering the conservatives. In 1900, he attacked the idea of biblical inspiration as it was then being understood and, in 1902, he published his most controversial study, *L'Evangile et l'Eglise.* Abbé Turmel did not begin to attack the Church in anonymous articles until after the turn of the century, though he had lost his faith earlier, in 1886. Le Roy, mathematician and lay theologian, did not issue his first attack on the traditional definition of dogma until 1905. In England, Tyrrell was not ordained until 1891; his difficulties with the authorities did not reach crisis level until 1901; and he was not dismissed from the Society of Jesus until 1906. In Italy, Minocchi's influence was first felt through a review he briefly edited, *Rivista bibliografica italiana,* which flourished and died within the three year period between March, 1896, and July, 1899. Murri was ordained in the year 1892 and became influential through two

periodicals for which he was responsible. *Cultura sociale* was first published in January, 1898, and *Vita nova* in February, 1895. Buonaiuti was
not ordained until the year 1903. Thus, the landmarks of this controversy
are all located within the two decades which straddle the turn of the
century.

It would therefore seem more appropriate to distinguish between the
movement which coalesced around 1890 and the broader impetus for
renewal which predated it. It is true that even von Hügel was willing to
speak of the latter as a "modernism,"[2] but plainly it was of such a vague
and diffuse character when compared with the movement itself that this
general and unspecific use of modernism is misleading. Nevertheless, the
Modernist movement was not without its context and antecedents, and
so some attention needs to be paid to this even though a full examination
of Church and society to which these sentiments of reform were a
response would take us far beyond the scope of this brief study.

The nineteenth century was in many ways a transitional period. It
is true, of course, that it was part of the broad stream of post-
Enlightenment thinking and thus perpetuated the intellectual revolution
which had started at the close of the seventeenth century. But, unlike the
century which had preceded it, the nineteenth found itself disenchanted
with rationalism and began to reach back for the forgotten verities which
the Romantics had cherished. This disenchantment spilled out across a
broad area of concern ranging from philosophy and religion to art and
politics. Basil Willey has deftly summarized the changing mood in this
way:

> In the first half of the eighteenth century life was conducted, on the whole, within a
> framework that was accepted as fixed and final. Fixities and definites were the
> order of the day: in society the appointed hierarchy; in religion, the Establishment;
> in Nature, the admirable order with its Chain of Being and its gravitational nexus
> which was mirrored in humanity by "self-love and social"; in art, the rules and the
> proprieties. The aim of politics, religion and philosophy was not to transform, but to
> demonstrate and confirm existing perfection; the aim of poetry was to decorate.
> But with the onset of the revolutionary age all this was altered; the fixities yielded
> to flux, mechanics to life and organism, order to process and the imaginative
> mouldings of the poets reflected on the ideal plane the great social changes which
> were proceeding on the material level. Life, growth and consciousness, those very
> mysteries which had never fitted comfortably into the mechanical scheme, now
> came into their own.[3]

In the early nineteenth century, these shifting concerns were given
brilliant exposition on the Protestant side by Friedrich Schleiermacher
(1768-1834), who is justly known as the father of modern theology. Living
at the nexus of two ages, buffeted by the currents that swirled around
him — Moravian pietism, Enlightenment rationalism, philosophical
Idealism, Germanic Romanticism — he sought to build a new theological
system. Schleiermacher was concerned to articulate Christian faith in

terms which "cultured" men would find attractive, for he was convinced, as the Catholic Modernists were later, that the chasm was widening between the new cultural concerns and the old Christian affirmations. In the absence of any intellectual reconciliation and adjustment between them, Christianity would become wholly isolated and culture would be seriously impoverished. In 1799, he published his study, *On Religion: Speeches to its Cultured Despisers,* in which he developed these ideas, showing that Christian belief did not require the negation of the emotional, aesthetic, and intellectual desires which were current, but was their finest realization. This book was followed by the more substantial and schematized study, *The Christian Faith* (1821-22), which developed the same general themes. Schleiermacher was not the only one to respond theologically to those mysteries mentioned by Willey: "life, growth, and consciousness." On the Catholic side, he was followed in different ways by Newman, Moehler, Blondel, and the majority of those thinkers who were classified as Modernists.

It would be quite incorrect to suggest that Cardinal Newman should be mentioned in the same breath as the Liberal Protestants. One of the most sensitive minds of the age, Newman recoiled from the ambiguities of the time and found refuge in the authoritarianism of Rome. His theology was developed within the intellectual and ecclesiastical structures of Roman faith; Protestant liberalism evolved largely in defiance of external structures and authority. Nevertheless, Newman did respond to the same issues as they, and he did accept a distinction, as they did, between that knowledge of God understood notionally and that grasped intuitively within the activity of the whole self. It was a distinction that was minutely explicated in that vast, contorted analysis of Maurice Blondel, published in 1893 and entitled *L'Action.*

Newman ultimately became a Cardinal despite his interest in the role of subjectivity in the formation of faith; this was a fact that did not pass unnoticed by the Modernists. Whether for good or bad motives, they aligned themselves with him. Tyrrell claimed that it was from the Cardinal that he had learned the core of his ideas and insisted in 1907 that *Lamentabili* had condemned Newman's ideas as well,[4] a charge that shocked Pope Pius X. Baron von Hügel, the co-ordinator of the Modernist movement who nevertheless escaped censure in 1907, was profoundly influenced, he said, by Newman's *The Grammar of Assent.*[5] Loisy, to the acute embarrassment of the Cardinal's more devout followers, declared Newman to be the greatest, if not the only great, thinker of the nineteenth century. Despite this enthusiasm for Newman's thought, Reardon is probably correct in saying that "to describe Newman as the 'father' of Modernism would be a reckless exaggeration, for the man who had taken anti-liberalism for his watchword would pretty certainly have been shocked by Modernist views."[6]

Some years after the Modernist debacle, Osborne wrote that Newman "was not a Modernist except in methods, although the Modernists carried off the honey from his hive."[7] The "honey" which the Modernists found in Newman was undoubtedly his recognition of "life, growth, and consciousness," those mysteries which were absorbing the attention of the nineteenth century and effecting an intellectual separation between culture and Christian faith. For if culture was concerned with growth and consciousness, Christian faith was still absorbed in fixities and definitions, the rules and the proprieties, mechanics and order, the existing perfection of Christian truth.

These new concerns caught the Church off balance. Throughout this period she was struggling, not so much for the mind of the age, as for her own existence. To some extent, though, the Church's problem was due not to the intellectual vigor of the nineteenth century but to the prolonged and damaging conflicts in which it had become embroiled within the European political structure. These conflicts had seriously weakened the Church, producing an uninformed antipathy to the intellectual issues posed by culture.

In France, for example, the spirit of nationalism had profoundly affected the internal life of the Church. For centuries, French kings had attempted to gain control of the Church through the means of appointments, but this ambition was finally realized in the Napoleonic Concordat of 1801. By this agreement Catholic faith was instituted as the nation's religion, but the right to nominate bishops was ceded to the State. Furthermore, the State assumed control of Church property and undertook to pay the clergy itself. Even after the demise of Napoleon I's empire and the restoration of the Bourbons, the Church continued to be governed by the Concordat of 1801. In 1830, however, whatever traces of the *ancien régime* which had been resuscitated by the Bourbons were rudely swept away by the July revolution which also had a bitingly anticlerical character. In the years which followed, the Church had to reckon with governments which encroached more and more on her preserves and private interests.

In this situation it was not surprising that a large number of Catholics viewed Gallicanism as dangerous and anti-Christian. Led by two noblemen, Vicomte de Bonald and Comte de Maistre, they came to favor a more powerful and centralized authority in the Church, one which could transcend nationalistic difficulties and provide a focus for culture and religion. An era of brotherhood, under benign papal rule, would thus begin. It is true that this dream was challenged by the Liberal Catholics, but Pope Gregory XVI showed beyond question in his *Mirari vos*, issued in 1832, that he was not in favor of the Liberal's counter-proposal. The separation between Church and State rested on insane and pernicious errors, he said. The problem, of course, was that this separation would emancipate the State from ecclesiastical control, even if it also freed the Church from the State's encroachments.

A fierce battle was joined in Italy, too. Pope Pius IX, once rumored to be sympathetic to the Liberals' ideas, was himself brutally ejected from Rome in 1848 when the city was besieged by revolutionaries. With the assistance of the French forces, he was able to return to the Vatican in 1850, but by then his liberal sympathies had completely evaporated. Nor was this the last struggle to engage the papacy in Italy during this time. In 1870, King Victor Immanuel surrounded the city and in the following year, 1871, the Law of Guarantees severely reduced papal political sovereignty. The vast theocratic powers which the popes had once claimed were now restricted in their realization to the seventeen square miles of the Vatican State. Pius IX vigorously protested this decision and together with four of his successors symbolically represented himself as a prisoner in his own state. The imprisonment was lifted by Mussolini in the Vatican Treaty of 1929. The issue of Church and State, however, seemed to surface everywhere in the nineteenth century, not only in France and Italy, but also in Germany, Austria, and other countries. Everywhere it distracted the Church's attention, sapped it of its vital energy, and forced it into a defensive posture.

This aggravation formed the background for Pius IX's celebrated bull, *Quanta cura*, which was issued in December, 1864, and to which was attached the Syllabus of Errors. The Syllabus in particular was aimed at those forces—political, social, and philosophical—which had ripped through society, tearing apart age old institutions, and had unleashed their pent-up fury on the Vatican itself. The Syllabus was the Pope's response to this situation; it was a repudiation of the whole drift of modern life; and it ended with the statement that it is an error to imagine that "the Roman Pontiff can, and ought to, reconcile himself to, and agree with, progress, liberalism and modern civilization."[8] In 1870, the First Vatican Council reinforced the tendency to look to a centralized and supranational authority by defining papal infallibility. The Council in effect distinguished between the fixed certainties of Catholic faith and the shifting ambiguities of modern civilization. A few years after the Council, in 1879, the bull *Aeterni Patris* was issued, adding strength and direction to Catholic faith, for this decreed once again that Thomistic theology should be more widely and earnestly studied. The result was the neoscholasticism which dominated the closing years of the century, frustrating and infuriating the Modernists.

Thus did the Catholic Church build her defenses against modern culture. It was not the defense of negotiation and accommodation but of inflexible rejection. Far from wanting to bridge the chasm that divided Christianity and culture, the Church seemed to welcome its growing isolation and the sense that it was swimming up stream. What adjustments she had made, the Modernists believed, were not only irrelevant but dangerously wrong. "The Episcopate," Tyrrell complained, "is busy about the papering of the attics while the basement is in flames."[9] It was in an attempt to restore the "basement," rather than to paper the "attics," that the Modernists, like Schleiermacher before them, developed a new theological position.

Modernism was an attempt to reach an intellectual rapprochement with contemporary culture.[10] A Catholic Modernist, therefore, was one who on the one hand was Catholic and on the other was part of modern civilization. But what did it really mean to be "modern" in this sense? G.K. Chesterton, with his customary vigor, said that the acceptance of modernity was little more or little less than snobbishness. It was, he said, the shabby pretension to being "in the know," in contrast to traditional Catholics who were not and never wanted to be. While traditionalists took refuge in the "citadel mentality," the Modernists were out in the world bravely holding aloft the banner of truth. The problem was that they had come to know too much to be able to believe as traditionalists did. But even Jean Rivière, who could hardly be considered a fellow traveler in the movement, saw the inappropriateness of this contention. The term "Modernist," he said, had only a vague relationship to the idea of modernity. Consequently, "the definition of it must be sought from its history and application since it cannot be discovered from the word itself."[11]

Rivière's suggestion that a definition be derived inductively from within the movement itself is undoubtedly correct, but it is by no means easy to implement. It implies that the movement had an intellectual consistency, tactical coherence, and a clear sense of direction. Modernists themselves stoutly denied the first two points, and on the third they contended that their sense of direction derived from a shared theological mentality, not from an identity in the conclusions to which their thinking led.[12]

The papal theologians who drafted *Pascendi* were contemptuous of this argument, seeing in it an attempt to deflect careful analysis because the Modernists feared that they would be exposed. The consistency which Modernist theology apparently lacked was duly provided by *Pascendi*. While it seeks a definition from within Modernist theology itself, it was nevertheless delivered in the formal logic of Scholastic reasoning of which, it must be said, Modernist writings were entirely devoid.

The task of compiling a *Summa fidei modernistae* was more complex than the papal theologians allowed. Their summary of belief they attributed to all Modernists. At the time and subsequently, however, there have been those who have claimed that the whole of it "was probably never accepted by any mind."[13] Was it possible, Maude Petre asked indignantly, "to blend in one condemnation the very distinct schools of thought and work?...how could they be classed under one appellation?"[14] Paul Sabatier was even more outspoken. Referring to the exposition of Modernist ideas which the Pope had given, he said:

> There is not in the land of the living a monster of the type he describes.... He is a nightmare creature with the voice of a lamb, the tail of a fox, the jaw of a wolf, and the wings of a seraph. What makes him particularly dangerous is that, though he is a compound of all errors, you can accuse him of no vice.[15]

Alec Vidler, utilizing Tyrrell's words, agreed that "there were as many modernisms as there were modernists."[16] Thus, to the Modernists at the time and to some interpreters since, the encyclical was regarded as a spiritual and intellectual atrocity.[17]

The accuracy of the encyclical's exposition has continued to be a matter of concern and debate. Following the protestations of the Modernists, it was again reviewed by the experts from the Congregation of Rites in preparation for Pius X's beatification. They concluded that he had been neither unfair in his charges nor unchristian in his actions.[18] It needs to be recalled, however, that important evidence was submitted at the time of the investigation which could have led to a modified verdict.[19] At least, it is clear that a definition of Modernism ought to be sought inductively from within the thinking of the movement itself and that the account given by *Pascendi* be accepted with caution.

According to Martin Green, Modernists worked along four quite distinct lines.[20] There were those like Loisy, Mignot, and Semeria who were particularly interested in biblical criticism and sought to fashion a new view of revelation consistent with the findings of contemporary biblical scholarship. Others like Tyrrell were particularly concerned with the traditional functioning of authority in the Church and sought to introduce changes consistent with modern self-consciousness. Le Roy was associated with a different concern, that of bringing official dogma into line with the exigencies of historical criticism. Finally there were those like Blondel who were working toward a new Catholic philosophy less Thomistic and more Augustinian. This analysis, of course, can be criticized for being simplistic. Tyrrell, after all, was as concerned about biblical criticism as he was about ecclesiastical authority, and Loisy's views on ecclesiastical authority were quite as distinctive as they were on the New Testament. Furthermore, there were some on the periphery of the movement who did not care to be called Modernists at all. Blondel, for example, perceived the drift of Loisyite theology very earlier on, dissociated himself from it, and then attacked Loisy rather forcefully. Nevertheless, the diversity of interest amongst the Modernists needs to be noted, for it means that any *Summa fidei modernistae* had to encompass in its summary the plethora of views which the Modernists entertained without being able to exonerate individual thinkers from holding views in fields where they lacked competence or interest. The whole of "modernist theology" was attributed to each Modernist.

It is important, then, to recognize that theological differences existed among the Modernists. "The Modernism of Tyrrell," said Maude Petre who, after all, was in a good position to judge, "is not that of von Hügel, or of M. Loisy."[21] Tyrrell himself protested:

> I represent myself alone. Abbe Loisy is impatient of me as a dreamer and mystic. Père Laberthonnière finds me guilty of occult scholasticism. One friend complains of my democratic, another of my conservative and aristocratic sympathies. With all due respect to the Encyclical *Pascendi*, Modernists wear no uniform nor are they sworn to the defense of any system; still less of that which His Holiness has fabricated for them.[22]

There are three matters in particular in which Tyrrell's views differed from those ascribed to him in *Pascendi*. First, the encyclical, which was published in 1907, failed to take account of Tyrrell's changed views on revelation which took place at the end of 1906. It ascribes to him as a Modernist the views which Loisy in particular had brought into prominence. In that "malheureux livre," as Blondel called Loisy's *L'évangile et l'église*, it is argued that Jesus did not intend to leave behind a static and unchanging "essence" or *depositum* of truth. What He gave the Church was a dynamic life which is ever in movement, each new phase superseding what has gone before it. The nineteenth-century expression of faith has eclipsed and indeed replaced the apostolic and first-century utterance of religious truth. Tyrrell, especially between 1904 and 1906, gave credence to this kind of view, and then he abruptly changed his mind. Subsequent to 1906, elements of this liberal notion were fused with the conservative view that biblical revelation is a fixed and unchanging *depositum* which is classical and normative and not open to development. *Pascendi* did not perceive his changed stance.

Second, in regard to dogma, the encyclical again seemed to have in mind Loisy's view. This was then taken as an adequate summary of what Tyrrell and the other Modernists held. The charge which was leveled against them was that they believed dogma was a product of the relative human mind and as such was always subject to change. Prior to 1907, Tyrrell had given indications that this is what he thought. Thus, J. Lebreton said that Tyrrell held that "dogma in its turn is no more than an intellectual representation aroused by religious emotions....It is not infallibly true; therefore it cannot be imposed of faith."[23] It is interesting to observe, however, that just prior to the publication of the Pope's condemnation, Tyrrell again changed his mind. He began to insist, quite against what he had held earlier, that dogma is a product of the Spirit, not of the mind. As such, it is infallible and unchanging. Whatever else he might have said about dogma which had given grounds for offense, this at least is the view of traditional Catholicism.

Third, *Pascendi* accused the Modernists of teaching that "secondary dogmas," to use Dilthey's term, were also to be considered as authentic dogmas. Tyrrell specifically denied that what was condemned was what he believed. Dogmas which explicate dogmas actually belong to the genre of theology, and not to that of dogma. Dogma is produced by the work of the Spirit, while theology is only the fruit of the mind. The former, therefore, is infallible; the latter is not. In making its charge, *Pascendi* seems to have had Le Roy's position in mind. It is fallacious to assume that Le Roy's Modernism was identical with Tyrrell's. The individuality of both these thinkers has been overlooked, and the result is an imperfect understanding of Tyrrell's position at least.

In seeking to define Modernism, then, it would appear necessary to aim for a looser statement than that offered by *Pascendi*. The emphasis needs to be placed more on Modernist mentality than on Modernist doctrines. Thus, Aubrey has said that "it is of the greatest importance to realize at the outset that modernism is a method and not a creed. Modernists are united by their approach to theology, not by their theological conclusions."[24]

Modernism was an apologetic venture. It was an attempt to build a synthesis between Catholic faith and the assumptions of secular thought. The price of such a synthesis was that Catholic faith had to be "pared down," Tyrrell said, but so, too, did secular culture. Nothing essential, however, would be lost to either side.[25] Through this rapprochement, society would find its fulfillment in Catholic faith and Catholic faith its realization in society. This was the goal of Modernism, and how it was to be reached varied from exponent to exponent. As a working definition, it is not necessary to say more, for then each theologian's "modernism" can be considered fairly on its own terms rather than on the basis of an abstract definition applied woodenly to all Modernists.

A consideration of Modernism in terms of its mentality and goals rather than its doctrines and conclusions thus allows us to examine Tyrrell's ideas in a fresh manner. All too often he has been treated as an English version of Loisy; continental scholars, in particular, are prone to treat him this way. Alternatively, the stereotype of the Modernist advocated by *Pascendi* has been considered an accurate representation of his ideas. In terms of an historical inquiry, however, we have no option but to reject these assessments, even if they are considered valid from an ecclesiastical point of view. Tyrrell must be allowed to speak for himself; his differences with other Modernists must be allowed to stand; and his innocence or culpability must be decided solely on the merits of his case. To ask for such freedom is novel in terms of the earlier studies carried out on Tyrrell in this century, but it is a freedom the Second Vatican Council said historians should have. Matters of an historical nature, it taught, "must also be presented from an ecumenical point of view, so that at every point they may more accurately correspond with the facts of the case."[26] It is the facts of the case that must now engage us.

Chapter Two

AN IRISH HEART, A GERMAN BRAIN

Across the sea from Wales lies a city which sometimes goes by its ancient name, the Town of the Ford of the Hurdles. It stands guard over both the Bay of the Irish Sea and the verdant hills which roll away behind it, a kind of sentinel and witness, the depository of seven centuries of history. This is Dublin. It is Eire's most important city, though it has never been a great commercial center. It is, however, a symbol, the embodiment of Irish defiance and Catholic faith. It was here that George Tyrrell was born and grew up.

The first Tyrrell to set foot on English soil was one of William the Conqueror's soldiers. Apparently he distinguished himself in his king's service, for he was rewarded with a piece of land alongside the river Avon in Hampshire. In time he gave his name to both a small hamlet and a large family. In years to come, part of the family moved to Ireland, though in two distinct migrations.

George's father William came from the line of the more recent Irish Tyrrells and in time became both the sub-editor of the *Dublin Evening News* and correspondent for *The Times* in London. It was by his second wife Mary Anne Chamney that George was born on February 6, 1861, the third in the family. On December 31, 1860, William died; thus his infant son George came into the world fatherless. This vacuum, however, soon was filled by George's older brother Willie who, as a child, had sustained a fall which had left him badly paralyzed. Brilliant but utterly frustrated by his confinement, he appears to have become embittered; everything Willie touched turned to ashes. Some of George Tyrrell's interpreters have seen in his childhood experiences and especially in his relationship to Willie an explanation of his attitudes and problems as an adult. Meriol Trevor, for example, has written:

> Tyrrell's accusations of the Society of Jesus may really be revelations of his own difficulties. Unlike his fellow novices he came into Church and Jesuit life all at once, with a disturbed, insecure childhood behind him, fatherless but inheriting his father's irascible temperament and influenced by his embittered clever elder brother. He would have had a difficult passage to maturity whatever life he had taken up. But when he was caught in a storm of self realization at the age of forty it was perhaps inevitable that he should react strongly against the intensive religious life he had lived in the Jesuit system.[1]

We need to be cautious, however, in attempting to psychoanalyze one long since dead and one whose partial recollections of his childhood were written long after the events. For if it is true that a child's environment may affect later attitudes, it is also true that later experiences may significantly affect what is recalled of the earlier years.

As a boy, George was sent to Rathmines School, but he proved to be an indifferent student. Middleton College, one of the more spartan boarding schools, was the place to which he was moved next. As he grew up, he began looking to the university in hopes of pursuing further studies, but these plans came to naught because he failed to gain the needed sizarship.

In the meantime, however, Tyrrell's religious interest had been quickened, first by his reading of Butler's *Analogy of Religion* when he was fifteen and then by his contacts with an Anglo-Catholic, Father Dolling.[2] Fascinated by Dolling's social work as well as by his faith, Tyrrell found Anglo-Catholicism to be little more than a stepping stone between the Protestantism of his home and the Roman Catholicism to which he now looked with quickened interest. His decision to become a Roman Catholic apparently happened almost on impulse after reading a book recounting the achievements of the Society of Jesus. On May 18, 1879, he was admitted to the Roman Catholic Church and immediately made arrangements to enter the priesthood.

Tyrrell's religious training began with brief, probationary periods of teaching in Cyprus and Malta, but it was completed back in England.[3] By 1882, he had finished his training as a novice. Throughout the early period, he remained idealistic about the Church. There was about him a guileless simplicity, an unashamed hopefulness, an exuberant optimism which must have been most attractive. But the reader of Tyrrell's *Autobiography* can detect signs of friction between Tyrrell and his Order which would later become very serious. We find him wondering, for example, how his fellow novices could equate mindless obedience to the Order with genuine religious commitment. Are faith in God and obedience to ecclesiastical authority really the same thing? This was a problem that haunted Tyrrell over the next decade, and his answer to it finally precipitated his excommunication.

Following his ordination in 1891, Tyrrell taught moral philosophy at St. Mary's Hall, Stonyhurst, but it was not a happy experience. In 1896 he had to be transferred to the Jesuit residence at Farm Street in London. Several reasons have been given for this move. Maude Petre suggested that the problem lay in the purity of Tyrrell's Thomism which discomforted his colleagues. He was turning their Jesuit students into Dominicans, they complained! It was also hinted that jealousy may have been a factor, for it is clear that Tyrrell had a charismatic bearing, a magnetic attraction, to which the students responded with enthusiasm.[4]

Whatever the reasons for Tyrrell's departure, the change in venue provided him with an opportunity to develop his ideas and, what is in retrospect more ominous, to put them into print. Apart from his books he published, in all, eighty-eight journal articles before his last publication in *The Month* in January, 1904.

Several years before Tyrrell's differences with his superiors became public knowledge, he had apparently sensed that a rift was developing; this is plain despite the fact that Maude Petre saw few difficulties prior to 1901. As early as 1897, he took the extraordinary precaution of having his book *Notes on the Catholic Doctrine of Purity* published privately. This was a tactic he used more than once in the years which followed. It circumvented the need for an *imprimatur*, a process that carried the potential threat of rejection and discipline, and it set out the first step in a defense against future difficulties. For if Tyrrell was guilty of publishing without Jesuit permission, the books, it could be replied, were restricted to selected recipients and therefore more like letters than books. Tyrrell, however, also resorted to the use of pseudonyms. Ernest Engels published *Religon as a Factor of Life* in 1902, and in the following year, *The Church and the Future* appeared under the name of Hilaire Bourdon. These, however, were palliatives, evasions; they could hardly be considered a *modus vivendi* for one living under the frustrating strictures of Jesuit authority.

In August, 1900, Tyrrell, under some pressure, left Farm Street in London for the quiet countryside of Richmond in Yorkshire.[5] In December of the previous year he had written an essay which others interpreted as an attack on the traditional doctrine of hell.[6] When the essay became a talking point and its author was identified as a Jesuit, Tyrrell's superiors became concerned. After some discussion and negotiation, it was decided that the best way to undo the harm which had been caused would be for Tyrrell to publish a letter which would put the offending essay in a slightly different light. He obliged, saying (as he had been asked to do) that there is a distinction between dogmas of faith or Catholic truths on the one hand and theological opinions on the other. The former are to be accepted without question, whereas the latter, into which category his essay fell, should not be, since no infallibility is attached to such writings. The storm passed, but only temporarily, for Tyrrell felt more frustrated than ever.

In March and May, 1901, writing from Richmond, he went into battle against the Joint-Pastoral which had just been issued and which asserted a traditional view of Church authority. Tyrrell attacked it both pseudonymously and anonymously.[7] In that same year he also became embroiled in a fierce debate over the censorship of his book *Oil and Wine*.[8] The censors were wary of passing it more out of their fear, it would seem, of its author's covert heterodoxy than for anything offensive

which was actually contained in its pages, although they did draw attention to some specific errors. They did agree to pass it after Tyrrell had
altered it, but then Cardinal Vaughan insisted on examining it personally
before giving his *imprimatur*. After a review of it, he decided to defer to
Rome, and so the manuscript was sent there. In due course it was returned with some offending passages marked. Not only had the book
undergone a triple censorship, but the views which the Roman censors
had questioned had already appeared in print in England under
Vaughan's *imprimatur*! Tyrrell was infuriated and threatened the Cardinal
with an *exposé*. His mounting frustrations over these negotiations were
expressed to Colley, the Provincial Superior of the English Jesuits, in this
way:

> If I joined the Society, as I did, solely to work for the cause of Catholicism; how
> shall I stay, if I am forced to regard her as one of the worst enemies of that cause?
> That is roughly how the case presents itself to me. If I married a harlot thinking her
> pure, I should feel bound, not to love or honor her, but to hold her to justice—for
> the risk is inherent in the contract.[9]

In the early months of 1901, just before this storm broke, Tyrrell suggested in several letters that he was contemplating writing an
autobiography that would enable him to put the pieces of his life
together again. Maude Petre and Bremond both hinted, and G. Daly[10] has
suggested, that Tyrrell had Augustine's *Confessions* in mind when he
finally produced this self-portrait. This may be so, but Tyrrell's purpose in
writing it was quite different from Augustine's. Tyrrell wrote his study in
1901 at a time of deep personal crisis, a time when his disaffection with
the Jesuit authorities was sharp and painful. He wrote, Meriol Trevor says
rightly, with the intention of finding himself.

Had his commitment to Roman Catholicism, no less than to the
Society of Jesus, been as firm and strong as he had thought originally?
This seems to be the question that had begun to afflict Tyrrell by the turn
of the century when he started to write the *Autobiography*. Consequently, his entry into the Society of Jesus is pictured as having occurred
almost wholly on impulse after reading Fèval's eulogy of the Order. And
his faith is presented as always being a rather unsure affair.[11] This interpretation and self-analysis prompted Wilfrid Ward to complain, as
Arnold Lunn did, that Tyrrell had deliberately read his later disillusionment into his earlier years. Ward took exception to the statement that
Tyrrell had felt himself devoid of faith at a particular point. Ward contended Tyrrell was always the very epitome of robust confidence and
strong religious faith during this period.[12]

Tyrrell's relationship to the Order continued to deteriorate during his
Richmond years. Events were moving swiftly in Europe. Loisy had been
disciplined by the Church, Turmel had abandoned his faith, and
Bremond, Tyrrell's friend and fellow-sufferer who in 1903 spent a few

months in England, had asked to be secularized in February, 1904. Tyrrell requested to be released from his vows in the following year, 1905, but before that happened he wrote a book which, all else failing, assured his final separation from the Society.[13]

Originally conceived as a pamphlet, *Letter to a Professor* was published privately in 1904 but reissued two years later as *A Much Abused Letter*. Brief though it was, innocent as it might have been in its conception, this book proved highly embarrassing to the Society. In December, 1906, the Milanese journal *Corriere della Sera* published an inaccurate and abbreviated translation of the book. The article was ascribed without further clarification to an "English Jesuit." The General of the Society inquired of Tyrrell whether he was the author. Initially, Tyrrell refused to admit or deny his authorship, suggesting that the question was irrelevant until his overall relationship to the Society was settled. A few days later, however, Tyrrell reversed himself, agreeing, as he said, to deal with the gnat before the camel, since the point of irritation at that moment, the anonymous article, could determine his future relation to the Society. Therefore, he admitted authorship, but qualified this admission by saying he had not seen the Italian translation. In January, 1906, Tyrrell was offered the option of publicly repudiating the article or of being dismissed from the Society. A letter written by Tyrrell was published, but since the authorities considered its penance unreal and insufficient, on February 19, 1906, he was served with his papers of dismissal.

Tyrrell's ecclesiastical position was ambiguous, to say the least, for although he had been dismissed by the Society, he had not been secularized. He was still regarded as a priest who required an ecclesiastical superior. But under whom could he serve?

During the years that Tyrrell was at Richmond he had contemplated leaving on several occasions. Von Hügel, a close friend and confidant who visited Richmond several times between 1902 and 1905, always insisted that before leaving he would need to find a bishop in whose diocese he could serve. This problem was simply intensified by Tyrrell's separation from the Society in 1906. Negotiations were protracted, complex, lightened occasionally by glimmers of hope, but in the end wholly frustrating. Tyrrell finally wrote an open letter to Cardinal Ferrata, and he requested Merry del Val to relay the letter to His Holiness.[14] In this letter he halted any further negotiations and elaborated on the indefensible practices and attitudes of which he had become a victim.

In fact, matters might have come to rest at this point had Tyrrell not been part of a larger movement. However, developments in Europe during the period of Tyrrell's frustrations with the Jesuit authorities were looking more and more ominous. In the following year, 1907, the storm broke. The Pope issued his encyclical *Pascendi* which was known, not inappropriately, as "l'encyclica ferox" by some theological students at the Germanic college in Rome. Michael de la Bedoyere has said that "of all major papal pronouncements in modern times this famous encyclical caused the most widespread discussion in the world."[15] Insofar as Tyrrell was a major participant in the movement at which it was aimed, he, too, felt the hot breath of ecclesiastical censure a second time.

The events which had preceded the publication of the encyclical had left Tyrrell tired, strained, and irritable. In this condition, he published his replies. Those appearing in England in *The Times* were more moderate than their European counterparts, but nevertheless they vigorously rebutted the encyclical. The Pope was accused of "going outside his sphere of judge of doctrine" to "condemn the characters, secret intentions, and motives of the modernists, extending to their persons that aversion which he, as a scholastic, so naturally entertains for their teaching."[16] The problem, Tyrrell said, was that of two interpretations of faith, one medieval and the other modern. The encyclical was "an attempt to gather the experiences of the twentieth century under the categories of the thirteenth."[17] Not even the "extreme theologians," he said, would regard such a document as infallible or authoritative. "It is a disciplinary measure preceded by a catena of the personal opinions of Pius X and his immediate *entourage*.[18] Two days later he wrote to von Hügel:

> With more time and quiet the shots could have been better aimed. Now they are delivered for better or for worse, and I leave the rest to God and Law. I know quite well that, not you, but others will find a certain shelter behind my enormities and will seem tolerable by comparison, especially as they will easily and sincerely be able to disavow me—much as Loisy makes Lagrange almost safe.[19]

Von Hügel was already aware of the dangerous predicament in which Tyrrell now found himself. On reading his letters in *The Times*, the Baron had written apprehensively that they were "very hot, vehement, and sarcastic." He added that he hoped that "this heat, which, in some places, is so apt, and in all is so understandable, may not, in the long run at least, deflect otherwise likely and winnable minds from the substantial content and real, final aim of your papers."[20]

Pascendi created considerable apprehension among Catholic thinkers in England, even those like Wilfrid Ward who were not altogether sympathetic to Modernism. Nonetheless, the English hierarchy closed ranks and affirmed its wholehearted acceptance of the encyclical. For Tyrrell, the writing was now on the wall. Negotiations regarding his future were carried on with Rome by the Bishop of Southwark. The outcome was that his case was reserved to the Pope and the sacraments were to be withheld from him. The word "excommunication" was not used with respect to these disciplinary matters, but this was, in effect, what had taken place.

Alone and disinherited, Tyrrell lived out his remaining two years in Storrington. In April, 1909, he wrote to Raffalovich saying, "my only wish is that my now declining years may be devoted to wider and more human interests than the wasted past."[21] Time, however, was running out. Three months later he was dead, the victim of Bright's disease.[22] His friend Bremond buried him in Protestant soil.

Tyrrell does not present a simple study for the historian. His personality was volatile; his views were often changing, either because his mood changed or because the circumstances forced him to take a different position. Indeed, on occasion, he could even hold totally different positions on the same day. Maisie Ward complained rather bitterly that he possessed "the power of being all things to all men to an extent that made him at times seem almost the echo of the man he had last talked with."[23] Tyrrell once admitted to von Hügel that this was the case, but he explained it as an unwillingness to dispute with his tongue. Anyone with self-assurance, he said, could "gull" him.

There was sometimes an element of incompleteness about Tyrrell's argumentation and thinking. His mind darted over the terrain, making lightning like stabs but failing at times to penetrate into the subject at great depth. He was constantly searching for new solutions to old problems, but he seldom lingered long enough with his ideas to produce a comprehensive answer. His thought is always suggestive, but not always compelling. He said that he denied "the scholastic's right to challenge him [the Modernist] for definitions and conclusions that are ever in the making and never made."[24] He went on to add, however, that "it would be wrong to suppose that because the growing ideas of modernist theology are necessarily incomplete and indefinable they are therefore worthless. For man, truth is an unending process of adequation, not a finished result."[25]

Outlining man's changing experience constituted, in Tyrrell's view, the work of the Christian theologian. It is not surprising, then, that with constant changes always in the offing, Tyrrell's friends and critics found it hard to pin him down on some matters. To a friend thus perplexed, Tyrrell said: "I plead very guilty to your charge of discontinuity—of too absolutely forgetting the things that are behind in reaching out to those that are in front. Each step negates rather than continues the preceding one."[26] At the end of his life, he made a similar remark:

> I think I can say with perfect sincerity that I am not very deeply attached to my system such as it is; and that I have assisted at its vivisection with a very dispassionate scientific curiosity. Had it expired under the process I should have buried it with great composure and gone in search of another.[27]

The old ideas of an unchanging truth and of an unchanging human nature were quite out of place in Tyrrell's world.

The incompleteness of Tyrrell's thinking and the cultured imprecision of his writing suggested to Percy Gardner that no one could compose out of his writings a "scheme of belief." The difficulties are, indeed, formidable. This is no doubt why Ratté has chosen to present Tyrrell's thought by means of a piecemeal description of the major writings as they appeared rather than as a composite whole. Not very much is ventured in this approach and, it seems, not very much is gained by it either.

While it is true that Tyrrell did not have a system in the scholastic sense, there was in the closing decade of his life an underlying consistency in his thought which seems to persist despite the surface variations which took place. Tyrrell even spoke of "my system." The consistency, however, derives from a steady approach to theological and historical problems rather than the finished results. This characteristic, though accentuated by his personality, was shared with other Modernists and, as it turned out, provided the principle of his theological methodology.

Chapter Three

DOING THEOLOGY

The nineteenth century gave little comfort to traditional theology. Indeed, it was a period in which theology in general was discomforted. Even Percy Gardner, who had less to fear from modernity than most, wrote in 1908 that no one "who really considers the signs of the times can cherish a light heart as regards the future of the Church."[1] But for the orthodox in particular these years brought numerous difficulties. In 1863, for example, Lyell's *Evidence for the Antiquity of Men* appeared and, in 1871, Darwin's *Descent of Man*. These volumes, representative of the new studies in archaeology and biology respectively, had an unnerving effect on the faithful. The fiction, widely and reverently held by many, that creation stretched back a mere six thousand years seemed to be disproved by these scientists with irritatingly little difficulty. Similarly, the new biblical scholarship also unsettled many of the orthodox, although the influx of German thinking, the source of all the grief, initially ran headlong into a solid wall of English prejudice. Canon Thirlwall, who translated Schleiermacher's *Critical Essay on the Gospel of St. Luke* in 1825, complained, "It would almost seem as if at Oxford the knowledge of German subjected a divine to the same suspicion of heterodoxy which we know was attached some centuries back to the knowledge of Greek."[2] English suspicion, however, was eventually overcome and in 1860 appeared *Essays and Reviews*, which proposed a new and more liberal stance on matters of biblical criticism. What was also alarming was that the challenge from science and biblical criticism, in different ways, received brilliant underpinning in the philosophical work of Kant and Hegel. Traditional belief, both Protestant and Catholic, was under assault from all sides.

Of the dangers surrounding Christian faith Tyrrell had no doubt. The Church, he said, "seems like some little Alpine village doomed by the slow resistless progress of a grinding glacier. Can she change now, even at the eleventh hour, and plant herself elsewhere out of the way?"[3] By refusing to budge from its old position, the Church was showing itself to be blind both to its obligations and its peril. Tyrrell was not alone in lamenting the Church's dismal response to the revolutionary ideas which were in the air, nor was he alone in seeking new answers to the problems they raised. His seeming capitulation, however, to the critics of Christianity, combined with his intemperate and even bitter denunciations of the Church, eventually made his excommunication inevitable.

At the root of the problem, as he saw it, was the scholastic mind-set which produced both an attitude of resistance to cultural change and a rigid way of conceiving of religious truth. The Church was then left floundering because it was constitutionally unable to deal with doubt. The scholastic knew everything, and doubt was always seen as a foe to be overcome by unflinching resistance. When values were in rapid transition, as they were in the late Victorian period, the psychology which resulted in the Church was one of uncertainty. This doubt was immediately categorized as a theological problem, rather than a cultural one, and attacked accordingly.

What the scholastic did not understand, Tyrrell countered, was that faith was not a mathematical verity that could be "known" with unclouded certainty. If there was light in it, there was also some darkness, because reason simply did not have the almost divine powers attributed to it by Tyrrell's traditionalist opponents. As he explained:

> Up to a certain point faith and doubt traverse the same path undistinguished and then they separate at its bifurcation and take one, each its own distinctive characteristic. In other words they have a common element in that deep sense of the insufficiency of the human mind to grasp and hold firmly the ultimate and vital truths of eternity.[4]

There is always an element of uncertainty in faith because of the intrinsic limitations of reason. Of necessity, man is *simul fidelis et infidelis*, "both believer and unbeliever." At the center of belief there is always a core of rational ambiguity. As the Gospel fades into the metaphysical twilight, it ceases to be an object to which the intellect can assent. Uncertainty of the mind, therefore, is not synonomous with the deeper doubt of the self, for reason itself takes us but a small way in the process of knowing.

But, more importantly, the scholastic approach actually deprived the Church of her sense of God,[5] a sense needed as much as ever before, given the difficult cultural and social circumstances in which she found herself. What this scholasticism had actually done, Tyrrell charged, was to slice reality into two halves, the natural and the supernatural, and had failed to establish adequate links between them. They became like two separate spheres whose purity was never violated by mutual contact. God was, therefore, contained within the supernatural realm, and His relation to the natural became obscure. The natural seemed to be evacuated of the presence of God, even though human nature retained some knowledge of His existence. In relation to man, scholasticism appeared to Tyrrell more like a metaphysical system of divine indifference than of love.[6]

God was regularly described, in deference to Aristotle, as the absolute and necessary Being who knows no limits, is tainted with no finitude, is removed from change. Neither creation as a whole nor man as a part can affect the divine reality in any way. In His essence, God is self-sufficient and self-subsistent. But does this view not dissolve the reality of God into a series of abstract and abstruse speculations? Tyrrell asked. How is it possible to experience such abstractions? If the scholastic doctrine did not facilitate an encounter with God, the Church was doomed and theology would become redundant.

Tyrrell's main difficulty with the traditional doctrine of God was not with its individual parts but with the way in which it was conceived. Scholastic speculations were in the same category as the scientist's classification into type and species. The scholastics' doctrine of God was like a dead beetle in a museum. "It is in men," Tyrrell countered, "that He, the hidden God, is to be sought, studied and loved—not in abstractions like Truth and Righteousness, but in concrete actions and will-attitudes."[7] It "is with the moral and religious effects of these possessions and inspirations [of religious experience] that religion is directly concerned, and not with the metaphysical nature of the agency to which they are due or with the mechanism of its operation."[8]

Again, Tyrrell argued that what man needs primarily is not theological information but that inward orientation towards the Divine upon which theology is called to reflect.[9] The existence of God is not a matter of "proofs" and "evidences" or cleverly devised arguments and clinically constructed propositions marshalled together into an irresistible argument that transport one into the divine realm. Said Tyrrell:

> Mr. Egerton complains that I assume, but nowhere prove, the existence of God. As I have said elsewhere: If God is what religion teaches, if He is to man's soul what light is to his eyes, or air to his lungs; if He is the correlate and coprinciple of this spiritual life, the medium in which the soul lives and moves and has her being, is it conceivable that we should hold Him merely by a slender thread of obscure reference; that it should be necessary to prove His existence before we begin to live a spiritual life? No; all we need do is to prove to men that they necessarily believe in Him; that they affirm Him in every movement of their spiritual and moral life.[10]

In what sense "men," which presumably might include atheists, "necessarily believe" in God, is an interesting question. Tyrrell neither substantiated nor defended his position. This statement is important for the stress which it lays on his inward, intuitive perception of God as opposed to the rational approach of the Thomists. It would therefore be correct to say that Tyrrell was a theist, not because this belief solved all of life's riddles intellectually but because it corresponded to and synchronized with the deepest appetites in human nature.

This shift in methodology, this distaste with the scholasticism that was so ascendant in the 1890s and early part of the twentieth century, seems to have been reached intuitively by Tyrrell. But he did formalize it in a series of rather tortuous steps by which, on the one hand, he came to adopt a Kantian epistemology (although always protesting that this was not the case) and, on the other, turned inward to find the basis for theology in what was fashionably being called the religious consciousness. Yet it would be quite wrong to see in Tyrrell, any more than in Schleiermacher, a theologian who was simply itching for novelty. The changes wrought in Tyrrell's thought life were forced upon him from the outside. They were the fruit of his anguish over the Church's predicament, the necessary adjustment, as he saw it, for survival in the new culture.[11]

The shackling of reason—an audacious move indeed given the prevailing atmosphere—was carried out because of Tyrrell's adoption of vintage Kantianism. Can reason take flight into the firmament and peruse God? Can reason adduce a divine existence meaningful to human life? Indeed not. Reason, first, cannot function independently of the stream of sensory data.[12] This presupposition plainly rules out any traditional metaphysics. Second, reason screens, organizes, and classifies the data received through the senses. It is interposed between the world as it is and what we know the world to be. This role, necessary if we are to know anything, means, however, that our knowledge is always synthetic and one step removed from reality.[13] To illustrate this point, Tyrrell said that no one expected to find beetles marching through the woods in ordered phalanxes according to the scientist's classifications. The classification into "type" and "species" is unnatural and its limitations must be recognized. A woodsman, in fact, has a far more accurate and comprehensive knowledge of life in the woods than does a scientist. Just as the scientist must allow the woodsman to fill out his knowledge of life as it really is, so the theologian—the scientific classifier—must allow the intuitive experience of the Church to correct his rational formulations. God Himself is very different from "type" and "species" classifications found in dogmatics manuals.

This contention leads, then, to the view that the intuitive "sense" of God, the consciousness of a presence which is other than human, is the stuff of which theology ought to be made. It may seem that Tyrrell's views at this point were so close to what Liberal Protestants were talking about that perhaps his eyes had been straying to the books they were so busy producing. That, in fact, is a plausible hypothesis, but it is also largely wrong. Although Tyrrell was rather careful about revealing the sources of his thought and almost seemed to cultivate an air of studied indifference towards other thinkers, it is incorrect to see him as a Protestant Liberal masquerading as a Jesuit Scholar. The route which he followed was quite different, although both he and the Liberal Protestants were reflexively responding to the same issues in culture.

Tyrrell moved toward this position instinctively rather than rationally,[14] but he did find a resounding affirmation of what he was doing in the philosophy of Maurice Blondel, whose writings he assiduously disseminated in England. Blondel, in his celebrated but extraordinarily difficult study L'Action, begins by analyzing the nature of dilettantism and pessimism.[15] The dilettante, Blondel argues, builds on the idea that at the center of life is a black, empty void. However, Blondel wants to show that the dilettante's perversion of Being into non-Being, his affirmation of nothingness, is actually a perverse acceptance of an existent Something. Blondel achieves this result by showing that in the dilettante's nihilism there is always a conflict between the will in its external life (volonté voulue) and the will in its internal relations (volonté voulante). For within the self-life there is a sense of the Divine, a vague perception of Something which transcends mere human experience. This sense cannot be extinguished, despite the fact that the manifest or external will functions on the flat plane of human experience where such a reality is unknown or, at least, unrecognized. The next steps in Blondel's argument are complex and need not be explicated, but the result is his contention that there is a logical route which can be taken from affirming the mere nothingness of appearances to recognizing the reality of universals, to the acknowledgement of the Something in which these universals co-inhere, to the final act in which this Something, the Divine, is willingly affirmed by a coherent act of the whole self.

The argument has not, however, answered the question as to how a man wills without actually willing to will. Beneath all volitional activity, Blondel argues, there is a Life whose presence is ultimately determinative on the will. This outcome is not reached however, without some conflict. The struggle itself exhibits an inner reality or Life without which there would not even be a conflict. This "one thing which is necessary," as Blondel terms it, cannot be disregarded or unknowingly violated, for all of man's native powers, his hidden depths, are allied to it. The more the pessimist or dilettante defies it, the more his actions exhibit it. The reality of the Divine is inescapable to man qua man. Summarizing Blondel's analysis, Dupré has said:

> Instead of pursuing the subject in its nature, its being, he considers it in its acting...
> for to Blondel the subject is act, and in acting, it discovers its own insufficiency as
> well as the need for a transcendent fulfillment. The religious problem, then, far
> from being superimposed on the problem of subjectivity constitutes the very centre
> of it.[16]

It is impossible to prove conclusively that there is an exact identity of position between Blondel and Tyrrell on this question. The agonizing contortions of Blondel's thought, the vast range of its activity, its discipline and thoroughness simply have no parallel in Tyrrell. Yet for different reasons, and by a much shorter route, Tyrrell appears to have arrived at the same conclusions. Tyrrell, like Blondel, also presupposed the existence of a "new life" which pervades the whole self-life. Like Blondel, he also affirmed that man's whole volitional activity, even if it is built on philosophical nihilism, is actually, in a perverse way, an affirmation of the existence of God. The intellectual denial has not, to be sure, coincided with the inward ontological affirmation. Denial, however, in this case is a meaningful form of affirmation, apparently for the reasons suggested by Blondel.[17]

The possession of a religious sense or consciousness, informed as it is by the Logos, is a universal phenomenon.[18] Writing of Catholicism, Tyrrell said:

> As for its paganism, it is undeniable that in its generic aspect as a religion, one of the great religions of the world, Catholicism is older than Christ; as old as humanity itself; as old as speech and language. Religions themselves, on their social and institutional side, are but the languages in which men hold converse with God. And these languages are of one family and one origin, human and divine; the work of God through man, and of man under God.[19]

In making this statement, Tyrrell apparently exposed himself to the charge which had often been made by Protestants that Catholicism was little more than a refined form of paganism. If the similarities were a cause of offense to the Protestant, they were a cause of delight to Tyrrell. He said:

> [The Protestant] delights to dwell on the analogies between Romanism and Paganism; we too dwell on them with delight, as evidence of that substantial unity of the human mind which underlies all surface diversities of mode and language, and binds them together as children of one family all who believe in God.[20]

Man, then, has always been to a greater or lesser extent "naturally Christian."[21] Christ's teaching was unique only in the sense that never before had the Divine been so clearly explicated or so strikingly manifested.

The idea that divine reality is in process and that the Church must refashion herself in accord with it was dangerous, for it could bring the charge of heterodoxy. Nevertheless, this process of refashioning, the Church's reflex to the inner mystery, Tyrrell called inspiration. He wrote:

> Inspiration means the progressive spiritualizing and refining of those gross embodiments in which man expresses his own ideas and sentiments about God. Thus the Eucharist is the last refinement of an idea originally gross and superstitious —the idea of sacrifice, partly refined in the law; further, in prophets [sic]; finally, in Christ. Christ's whole "revelation" was little else but a further correction of the better sort of religion which he found in Israel.[22]

Christianity was not something imposed on man from "above," as if it were some alien commodity which he had hitherto lacked. Rather, one can perceive in the very genesis of mankind the origins of Christianity. These primitive workings of the Divine were to expand through the centuries, reach some kind of peak in Christ, and then extend beyond into the world and into the future. Said Tyrrell:

It was not pure Judaism; but Judaism reformed and spiritualized by the prophets; universalized by the philosophy of Alexandria; perfected in both respects by Christ; preached and proclaimed explicitly as a world religion by St. Paul, that was rejected by the synagogue and received by the Gentile world, already prepared to welcome a religion of humanity, a synthesis of all other religions.[23]

What is not clear is how this unfolding of God is to be considered. Is it that we come to understand more of what was always there or is there an actual change in part of the reality of God? It would seem most likely that Tyrrell was merely arguing for the first option, but there is some suggestive, if inconclusive, evidence that he might have been moving towards the second position. The first is compatible with the notion of doctrinal development as elaborated by Newman, but the second is by traditional standards decidedly heterodox.

Tyrrell sometimes denied that he was a mystic. To Raffalovich he said, "inspite of my intellectual appreciation of mysticism, I am constitutionally the least mystical of beings, and have got a hard vein of rationalism running down my spiritual spine."[24] Nevertheless, the elements of a mysticism that is at once medieval and modern are clearly present in his thinking: the denial of absolutes, the belief in the inadequacy of reason in penetrating and comprehending the being of God, and the persistent concern with intuitive perception of the self that eludes the grasp of reason. To a friend he confessed that his conception of God was:

reduced to a dialogue with that (so evidently) spiritual and personal power within me which claims, every moment, my absolute worship and obedience; which is as real and self-evident to me as the most constant impulses of my 'nature' with which it is in perpetual and sensible conflict. My imagination is quite cured of the outside God, for I feel that the inward spirit pervades and transcends the whole universe and reveals to me but an infinitesimal fraction of its Will and End and Truth and Nature.[25]

Some of these ideas emerged in what was perhaps Tyrrell's most important essay, "The Relation of Theology to Devotion."[26] In this essay he sought to distinguish between revelation and theology. Revelation is that intuitive knowledge of God given to man in the depths of his self-consciousness; theology is the reflection on this consciousness, the intellectual response to it. Tyrrell argued that these two forms of knowledge are entirely different. Not least among their differences is that revelation is ever in process of movement and change, whereas theology is always attempting to freeze this development at each point. No theological form ever adequately "captures" revelation. Indeed, the problem of obsolescence is nowhere more evident than in the theological enterprise! Consequently, it can never be said that revelation is ever finally "given." Thus, Scripture and tradition must be read as theology rather than revelation, and as such they are always open to revision.[27]

Knowledge of reality, then, is not "contained" in any receptacle. It is not readily and easily amenable to those who are casual, slothful, and superficial. Rather, it is won in the arduous and painful journey which the human spirit makes as it moves toward the Transcendent.[28] This goal is like an ever receding shadow, a road which has no end. But something within man compels him toward this "end that is as yet unknown."[29] Because the end to which man moves is always obscure, it can never be seen as an object of *assensus intellectualis*. Man must ever be *simul fidelis et infidelis*. The capacity of faith never coincides with the whole substance of the divine object of faith.

The obscurity of the end towards which the self is moving focuses all the attention on the religious stance in the present. The *act* of faith rather than the *object* of faith assumes the importance. Truth, Tyrrell might almost have said, is subjectivity.

An alternative way of conceiving God was thus suggested by the Irish Jesuit. Its novelty lies less in its substance than in its method. Refusing the traditional separation between natural and supernatural, Tyrrell sought to integrate them. It is, therefore, paradoxical that even when his thought seemed to be leaning towards a "panentheism,"[30] when he might even have been caught up in a form of Spinoza-like "God intoxication," he still had relatively little to say about the Being of God.[31] The answer to this enigma lies in an understanding of the strictures which his methodology placed on him. His theology was necessarily anthropocentric, but, at the same time and for this reason, it was, in his view, theocentric. Tyrrell could speak of God only when he had first spoken of man; in speaking of man, he had begun to speak about God. Man, therefore, is the means of approach to God and the means of communication from God. Only through man can God be understood, for man is the bond between the temporal and the eternal. Thus Tyrrell had more to say about man than about God. But, given the radical insufficiency of reason to understand the Divine depths, could it ever have been otherwise?

It is important to observe that these ideas were for more than a mere reflection of Tyrrell's interest in mysticism; they constituted a theological methodology, a way of thinking about God, human nature, the Church, and the world which were pioneering and novel when judged by the expectations of his Church. Because it was a method, everything that he thought and much of what he did were outgrowths of it. Consequently, it is necessary in the chapters which follow to examine the implications of his method for Church and revelation. The actual outworkings of this approach need, however, to be seen immediately, and three matters are selected for brief perusal by way of illustration. These are, first, the question of religious language; second, that of his troubled Christology; third, the issue of the "anonymous Christian."

First, then, the problem of religious language. This problem was latent in many of his statements about human reason as, for example, when he said that the mind's categories are drawn from the empirical world and therefore "it has no proper idea of the transcendent Whole and its relations, nor can it determine how the spirit in each of us is related to the universality of Spirit."[32] Again, he said:

> To realize clearly the often comparatively loose relation between faith and its intellectual expression; to understand that a language derived from, and primarily adapted to, the visible world can never be adequate to the utterance of the invisible, is to have delivered one's soul from a whole brood of idle fears and fancies, and to have risen above the storm-level to a region of untroubled serenity.[33]

How loose, we are forced to ask, is this relationship? On what grounds can the transition from empirical to non-empirical take place? How is God-talk possible?

An important distinction for which Tyrrell argued was that between facts and values. By and large, modern theology has also followed this line of thought. Value statements, it is said, cannot have factual bases and religious affirmations cannot be simultaneously scientific ones. This position obviously disallows metaphysics, at least in a traditional sense.

Tyrrell, however, denied that he was antimetaphysical and assumed that a transition from the empirical to the metempirical could be made.[34] Precisely how this occurs is not always clear,[35] but his solution, in so far as it is developed, is very interesting. He seemed to reject the idea, which was later advocated by Carnap, that language is merely a technical system adapted to and derived from the sensory world. There is more to language than this. It has a "soul" no less than a "body," "substance" no less than "envelope."[36] This approach would seem to bring Tyrrell nearer to Heidegger's notion that the purpose of the language is to distill meaning from experience and in the process become the bearer of Being. Transferring this idea from philosophy to theology, religious language could be described as sacramental. This is the notion which Tyrrell held.

Religious language was, for Tyrrell, necessarily symbolic because the mind has no direct access to God. Starting with this premise, it is not surprising that Tyrrell advocated a view of language which is also remarkably similar to that of Paul Tillich. First, religious symbols always point beyond themselves, but to what they point we are uncertain. Second, a symbol such as the incarnation or resurrection cannot be created at will.[37] Its creation occurs beneath the level of consciousness as a result of man's inner union with the Divine. There is an inevitability to Christian symbols and, although the reality to which they point is uncertain, they must be allowed to have a regulative effect on Christian life. Third, these symbols not only point beyond themselves but also mediate divine reality to the Christian community. In this sense they operate sacramentally.

Language, then, has two aspects to it: there is the inner spiritual reality, its "soul," and there is the "body" or the outer aspect—the myth, legend, story and symbol in which spiritual reality is communicated. The "body" is comprehended intellectually, but the "soul" is grasped only intuitively. Of these two aspects, it is the "soul" which is obviously more important:

> The 'Spirit' of Christ does indeed depend on certain truths and apprehensions by which it is generated and characterized, but they are truth of immediate intuition and contact, and not those symbols of the sensuous imagination nor those concepts of the natural understanding into which such experiences have been translated for purposes of communication to them.[38]

The distinction Tyrrell wanted to make was between "Christ's vision and the expression of that vision; the latter was but a rude sketch or suggestion of the former in terms and conceptions familiar to fishermen of Galilee."[39]

The work of the critic, therefore, is to accept this distinction and then, by utilizing the symbol, to try to recapture the essence of that inner truth which is being conveyed. As a result, none of the main terms of traditional faith should be taken at face value. All need to be demythologized and explored. For example, Tyrrell concluded that Jesus' Messiahship really symbolized not His divine status but His experience of His "own relationship to God;"[40] incarnation taught the immanence of God in all men but in particular in Jesus;[41] atonement was really the expression of man's sense of alienation from God; resurrection was merely an apostolic expression of appreciation "of Him who had opened their spiritual eyes and ears;"[42] *parousia* taught man's need to be related to the eternal world. The early Christians, he concluded, erred in their belief of a literal return of Christ because the teaching about a literal *parousia* was confounded with the spiritual reality of which it was the symbol.[43]

Given this general framework we come, second, to a consideration of his Christology. Was Christ God-incarnate, the second person of the Trinity, robed by and joined to human flesh? If the "vision" of him which the apostles had was blurred, and necessarily so because of the limitations of reason, can anything be said about Christ other than the effect which he had on the Church? Is the apostolic Christology merely a mirror of apostolic consciousness or is it a reflection of who Christ actually was?

It might be tempting to read Tyrrell—despite his overt hostility to Protestant Liberalism—as a follower of Schleiermacher, as one who saw in Christ simply the quintessential religious man whose God-consciousness had become sufficiently potent to become an existence of God in him. At times Tyrrell came close to saying this, and in 1909, he admitted to von Hügel that he had been dominated by the "Liberal-Protestant Christ," but he was never fully satisfied with it. Christ, he once countered, differed in *kind* and not merely degree from other men,[44] and although he gave a symbolic interpretation to the resurrection, he found it hard to jettison the thought that Christ had risen from the grave. When Loisy proposed that the body had rotted in the grave, Tyrrell wrote to von Hügel:

> I am aghast at the Loisy escapade and, since he is not a fool, puzzled as to his motives. All that interests us is to know that the resurrection was not fleshly; after that 'the flesh profiteth nothing.' There is no additional unorthodoxy in this statement about the fate of the body; but there is additional shock; or what is worse, a decided touch of cynicism.[45]

He took up the same rather ambivalent position with respect to the virgin birth in another letter to his friend von Hügel.[46] That he affirmed a Christology less full than Chalcedon's is beyond doubt, but he was nevertheless reluctant to dispense with the historical veracity of the incarnation, atonement, and resurrection, not because he himself actually held these to be historical, but because their retention was necessary for the preservation of the "real" belief. Just as one cannot have a soul without a body, so one cannot have the significance of the incarnation without maintaining the tradition of the virgin birth, untrue as it might be.

Third, Tyrrell's methodology led him to affirm the existence of what today are called "anonymous Christians," and the route to this affirmation then was very similar to what it is now. His reasoning was as follows. Given the limitations of reason in religious matters, its inherent inability to yield a full harvest of knowledge in this domain, a person's real beliefs may be very different from his rational account of them. Tyrrell explained that the Divine within offers "no information beyond 'yea' and 'nay' to our questionings."[47] Man must continually experiment in bringing his rational schematizations into accord with the impulses of Divine life. This process is long, difficult, and uncertain; its very uncertainty is what forces us, Tyrrell said, to distinguish between conscious and unconscious truth. Thus he wrote:

> a man might have great faith in the Church, in the people of God, in the unformulated ideas, sentiments and tendencies at work in the great body of the faithful, and constituting the Christian and Catholic 'Spirit', and yet regard the Church's consciously formulated ideas and intentions about herself as more or less untrue to her deepest nature; that he might refuse to believe her own account of herself as against his instinctive conviction of her true character.[48]

In short, the theologian's task is that of bringing the Church to a greater and more authentic level of self-consciousness. What Tyrrell was really trying to do, of course, was to give to will and intuition the prominence which had traditionally been given to reason. By the will, man has access to the realm of spiritual reality;[49] by reason, he has contact only with the "world of appearances."[50] "The reach of the heart," Tyrrell said, "is more extended than the reach of the mind; that it can penetrate to a depth of soul, where light fails the intellect; that it can touch what the mind cannot see."[51] The outcome of this line of reasoning is that belief can lie within unbelief. One can even encounter within the same person an existential faith concealed within a rational atheism. This is a startling proposition, but not so heterodox that the Second Vatican Council was unable to endorse it.

However intemperate or misshapen Pius X's encyclical *Pascendi* may have been, it was accurate in its depiction of the philosophical assumptions with which Tyrrell, as one of the Modernists who was condemned, functioned. The encyclical declared that "agnosticism" and "vital immanence" provided the main structure for the Modernists' methodology. According to the first principle, reason was restricted to phenomena, with the result that any specifically Christian schema of interpreting the world had to be yielded as did traditional metaphysics; according to the second principle, religion arises from the "sub-consciousness" and God is perceived merely as that which corresponds to an inner appetite or "sense." These notions produced the Modernists' "most absurd tenet," namely that within every religion are the shadows of an authentic Divine presence. These are the "ravings," it declared, by which these audacious reformers were seeking to change the church!

How St. Pius X might have viewed the Second Vatican Council if he lived on into the present age is a somewhat impious speculation, but it is a question that ought not to be avoided. We must seek to explain how the Church can today openly and joyfully affirm what it so sternly and sorrowfully repudiated only yesterday.

It is quite true, of course, that insuperable difficulties stand in the way of a point by point comparison of Tyrrell and the Second Vatican Council. The age in which he wrote was quite different from that in which the Council functioned; the questions which are addressed are different; the solutions which are offered are often different; and, worst of all, the Conciliar documents are a compromise reached by two thousand bishops in fourteen months of work, whereas Tyrrell's works are the fruit of one mind written over many years. Yet even given these difficulties, it is odd to note that the Council seemed to adopt a methodology that at least ran parallel to his and produced results that were at points startlingly similar. Two of these points of convergence, I suggest, are, first, the changed relationship between "nature" and "super-nature" and, second, the role played by "religious consciousness."

First, the old distinction between the natural and supernatural about which those who were scholastically oriented discoursed at great length has been profoundly modified in the documents of the Second Vatican Council. This modification, I believe, is seen in a number of places but quite obviously in the notion of sacramentality, which was also one of Tyrrell's favorite ideas.

The impetus for this theme, proponents say, came from patristic theology. Latin theologians were inclined to translate the Greek word for mystery, *mustērion*, by the Latin *sacramentum* from which our English word *sacrament* is derived. The idea of sacrament, then, is closely related to mystery. More particularly, it has reference to the visible dwelling place through which God's glory and saving knowledge are manifest. In patristic theology, the word *sacramentum* was primarily applied to Christ because, by means of His humanity, it is said, the invisible reality of God has been effectively communicated to men. In Christ, one sees not only a symbol of God's redemptive plan but also its means of realization. In a secondary and derivative sense, the Church, which is Christ's body, ought also to be regarded as a sacrament.

In the opening statement of *Lumen Gentium*, the Church is described as a sacrament because it is a "sign" of God's presence in the midst of human life. It is also a visible manifestation of man's intimate union with God and of the corresponding unity of the human race.[52] Moreover, this union and unity apparently center in Christ, through whom God's eternal plan to encompass all nations in the fellowship of salvation is made known.[53] By her union with Christ, the Church has become "the universal sacrament of salvation" for all nations, foreshadowing their ultimate unity and revealing the christological basis on which it will be realized.[54]

The Church's role as the "sacrament of the world" is not merely symbolic. She does not merely point to Christ; she also effects a Christ-ward union. In her sacramental role, the Church is "an instrument for the achievement of such unity."[55] Christ uses her "as an instrument for the redemption of all."[56] The parallel between the Church and the humanity of Jesus is inescapable. The Logos now uses the Church to effect salvation even as He formerly used the man Jesus. There are difficulties in the analogy, and the Council was clearly aware of them. The Church's humanity is soiled by sin, whereas that of Jesus was not; divinity and humanity were joined in the Person of Christ in hypostatic union, whereas in the Church they are not. But in referring to this parallel, the Council evidently wanted to stress God's effective use of Christian humanity in mediating divine salvation to the world.

Having stated the principle of sacramentality in general, the Council then made particular applications of it. Hierarchical orders, for example, were redefined in terms of sacramentality,[57] as were Scripture, tradition,[58] and the liturgy.[59] Some of the Council fathers were disturbed by these actions. After all, the Council of Trent did pronounce an anathema on anyone who allowed that there were more than seven sacraments. On Cardinal Ruffini's suggestion, therefore, it was decided to reaffirm the distinction between sacraments and sacramentals[60] and to refer these seemingly novel uses of the word *sacrament* to the latter category. The distinction is a semantic one only, made in deference to the heavy load of tradition by which the Council was in part bound. The Council has evidently broadened its notion of sacramentality, seeing in the Church the general realization of this principle and in the seven traditional sacraments its particular application. The whole People of God is the habitation, sign, and instrument of God's saving life.

It is of interest to note that one of Cardinal Ruffini's reasons for rejecting the application of sacramentality to the Church was its historical pedigree. George Tyrrell, he said, was among those who had utilized this idea, and *Pascendi* had duly condemned it. Ruffini was quite correct in his observation. Tyrrell did believe that there is a gradation of sacramental effectiveness which is at its lowest point in physical nature, is more intense in the Church and Scripture, and reaches a climax in Christ. On each level of existence—physical, ecclesiastical, and christological— divine reality is both symbolized and communicated by these visible means. With minor differences, it is these very ideas which have reappeared in the Council documents, and, one suspects, for the same reasons.[61]

At the root of the new emphasis on mystery is a pessimism regarding the value of reason in religious matters. While Tyrrell was explicit in his rejection of scholasticism and in his formulation of the voluntarism which was to take its place, Vatican II has merely bypassed without comment the Hellenistic framework into which Christian thought has been integrated. It is simply insufficient, the Council seemed to say, to penetrate the Christ-event with any great profundity.

This conclusion is almost certainly related to the distinction proposed by the "Nouvelle Théologie" of the 1940s, and apparently accepted by Pope John, that there is a difference between essence and historicity.[62] To assume that the Christ-event and man's understanding of it are in any sense identical is to suggest that man has transcended his creatureliness, that he has escaped the relativities of time. Between any event and man's understanding of it is interposed the obfuscating filter of humanity. It is this radical insufficiency of the mind which is underscored by the eloquent discussion on mystery and sacramentality.

It would not be incorrect to see, lying over this discussion, the long shadow of Immanuel Kant. If Tyrrell followed some Kantian assumptions, so, it might reasonably be deduced, did some of the Council fathers. The result of their approach is that the old distinction between the natural and supernatural is being steadily erased. This fact also emerged in one of the later elaborations on the People of God theme, namely, eschatology.

Traditionalists who have a Hellenized view of God have frequently been accused by progressives of having a universe made up of two layers, nature and supernature. Traditionalist eschatology, it is claimed, was largely thought of as the transition from the former to the latter. In the nature of the case, the transition was thought to take place upwards. The axis of eschatology, it might be said, was a vertical one.

There are hints, and substantial ones at that, that the axis of the Council's eschatology lies horizontally, although in certain places of some of the old ideas were endorsed. But it does seem clear that the Council endorsed the progressives' idea, later extended by Schillebeeckx and Baum,[63] that secular life encases the reality of God and may even facilitate a fresh encounter with Him. The old antithesis between the sacred and the secular, God and the world, is strangely absent from the documents. The two spheres of reality are far more closely integrated than they were in traditional thought. The goals of eschatalogical hope, therefore, are considered "beyond" rather than "above;" heaven is not an ethereal sphere outside of time but will be realized as a climax to the historical process. This teaching emerges, for example, in the following passage:

> For after we have obeyed the Lord, and in His Spirit nurtured on earth the values of human dignity, brotherhood and freedom, and indeed all the good fruits of our nature and enterprise, *we will find them again* [my italics].... This will be so when Christ hands over to the Father a kingdom eternal and universal.[64]

Barnabas Ahern has admirably summarized the significance of this teaching:

> What really matters is the tremendous truth affirmed by the Council that all worthwhile human activity is part of the creative plan of God and of the redemptive mystery of Christ who died that he might re-establish all things and transform them into the perfect eschatological kingdom of his Father. The whole world—the heavens and the earth, the vast oceans and verdant fields, the tangled bush of Africa and the trampled streets of New York, men of all colors and of all backgrounds—all that God has made is alive with an *élan to God*.[65]

A thorough-going secular theology or process theology is not to be found in the Council documents. But there are hints, undeveloped as they are, which point in this direction. Some of the ideas of Tyrrell also pointed in this direction. His rejection of Scholasticism with its Hellenization of the doctrine of God finds its echo at Vatican II. A dynamic, as opposed to a static, view of God, the creative process, and history is to be found both in Tyrrell and in the conciliar teachings. A new view of the relationship of the natural to the supernatural is another point of similarity, as is the wide ranging application of sacramentality. Insofar as this identity pertains, it is possible to argue that the Council has reiterated some aspects of Modernist theology.

The second area of convergence is the "religious consciousness" as an important methodological factor in the doing of theology. According to one aspect of conciliar teaching, man *qua* man has religious awareness. A *numinous*, a sense of mystery, pervades his existence. From "ancient times down to the present, there has existed among diverse peoples a certain perception of that hidden power which hovers over the course of things and over the events of life." The Council went on to say that "such a perception and such a recognition instill the lives of these people with a profound religious sense."[66] We are to explain this sense also by the fact that in the incarnation "the Son of God has united Himself in some fashion with every man."[67] In other words, the self-experience of mankind would have been different had the incarnation not taken place. This inner sense, this "supernatural existential" to use Rahner's phrase, is a prereflexive and intuitive knowledge of the presence of God "in" all human life. It is the *sine qua non* for that more specific and thematized knowledge which theologians are to develop and the Church is to teach.

The traditional tendency to identify the Kingdom of God exclusively with the Church of Rome, therefore, is no longer tenable. The Church of Rome does not exhaustively contain and enclose divine reality. God is perceived and known outside the confines of Catholicism. Separation from Rome does not mean separation from the truth; it means merely that one is separated from the truth in its fullness.

To articulate this shift in stance, the Council developed a subtle vocabulary. Its aim is to convey the notion that there are degrees of membership in the People of God, gradations of proximity to the center of all reality which is Christ. Religious ideas, therefore, were presented as a series of concentric circles. At their center is Christ, and the first circle around Him is the Catholic Church. Catholics are said to be "incorporated" in Him and their incorporation is "full."[68] Catholicism, however, does not completely enclose the reality of God within its structures; He is also perceived and known outside of Catholicism. In fact non-Catholic Christians are said to be "joined" to Christ.[69] Their Christian experience is not as full as those who are Catholic. Nevertheless, it is not empty either, as traditional Catholics had sometimes contended. Moving still further from the center, we encounter theistic but non-Christian religions such as Judaism and Hinduism. They were said to be "related"[70] to Christ. Finally, even atheists may find salvation despite their state of non-belief.[71] Explicitly they may be atheistic, but implicitly they may be Christian in the depths of their being. A man's real beliefs, as Tyrrell once intimated, are subconscious rather than conscious. To sum up, no one across the whole spectrum of religous belief is wholly identified with Christ (not even the Catholic) and no one across the whole spectrum of existence is wholly separated from Him (not even the atheist).

The Second Vatican Council reached this position by much the same route as Tyrrell had done. The Council was willing to explore subjective religious experience even if it meant minimizing the importance of objective ecclesiastical teaching. This point was well explained by B.C. Butler when he said:

The Constitution on the Church... in its chapter on the People of God, opens its discussion of salvation by a primary affirmation that 'whoever fears God and does what is right is acceptable to God' (n. 9). Only after laying down this principle does it proceed to teach that the objective means of salvation are given by God in the People of God, that is, the Church. This inversion of the traditional order of thought may be taken as a shift in emphasis from objective to subjective. Salvation is, for the individual, radically dependent rather on subjective good intention than on external ecclesiastical allegiance.[72]

With the importance of the visible Church waning in matters of salvation, at least one tenet of traditional belief needs to be modified, namely, the dictum that *Extra ecclesiam nulla salus*. Butler has shown how the formula might be reinterpreted, arguing that in people of different religious views as well as in those who have none, "Christ is (anonymously) at work, and that in them also the Church, *extra quam nulla salus*, is transcending her own visible limits."[73]

Without knowing it, the Council actually reproduced Tyrrell's position with extraordinary precision. For Tyrell had argued that

in these days the thoughtful Catholic no longer regards his Church as a sharp-edged sphere of light walled round with abrupt and impenetrable darkness, but rather as a center and focus from which the light of religion, spread over all ages and nations, shades away indefinitely in varying degrees with that darkness that can never wholly conquer it. He cannot stand so far from the focus as not to share some measure of its influence, however qualified; in a word he cannot suffer complete, inward, spiritual excommunication.[74]

In these words, Tyrrell anticipated all the ideas endorsed by the Council: that all men sustain a Christward relation; that there are gradations of proximity to Christ; that Catholicism is the nearest to Him and possesses the most truth; finally, that the inversion of traditional values whereby the subjective aspect of belief becomes more important than the objective (ecclesiastical) means of structuring that faith. At the same time, it must be said that there are differences between Tyrrell's views and those accepted by the Council. These differences, however, mainly arise in explaining *how* men are related to Christ. There is no question *that* they are. Tyrrell developed his theological anthropology fairly explicitly and with a measure of completeness; the Council, by contrast, was notably silent about the anthropological base on which the Constitution *Gaudium et Spes* in particular is built. It contented itself merely with some general references to man's ordination to a supernatural end and his inner illumination by the Logos. But if the premises beneath the new Catholic thinking are obscure, the results are nevertheless remarkably Tyrrellian.

In 1907, Pius X took a position which is seemingly critical of what Vatican II has approved. In rebuking the Modernists, he complained that "in the conflict with different religions, the most Modernists can maintain is that the Catholic has more truth because it is more vivid, and that it deserves with more reason the name of Christian because it corresponds more fully with the origins of Christianity."[75]

The ecclesiastical ramifications of this convergence between Modernism and what G.C. Berkouwer has called the "New Catholicism" are beyond the scope and interest of this study. What is of concern is that Tyrrell's role as an almost prescient formulator of things to come be recognized. It is an old adage, perhaps cynical but invariably true, that the victors write the history. And the "history" we have of the period of Modernism is almost without exception fiercely antagonistic to him.

What is now plainly at stake is not so much the facts but rather their meaning. This meaning has both a personal and an ecclesiastical dimension. On the one hand, we have to ask whether the construction placed upon Modernist intentions by its opponents was accurate. In some instances, at least, we shall see that it was not. On the other hand, we need to ask afresh, given the light now shed by the Second Vatican Council on these debated issues, whether the theological construction placed on Modernist ideas was true. In many important instances, we have to say that today the interpretation would have been quite the opposite of what it was at the turn of the century. For the Church, this raises the question of how quickly authentic doctrine can legitimately develop into its antithesis; for the historian, it poses the question as to whether Tyrrell was a prophet before his time. And that, in turn, suggests that a fresh reconstruction of Modernism, at least in its English expression, might now be appropriate.

Chapter Four

REBUILDING THE CHURCH

Tyrrell's attitude to the Church was probably the least complicated and the most fascinating aspect of his thought. He came to be opposed to the organized Church, arguing that it was misconceived in its biblical origins and misshapen in its historical development. And, in moments of raging intensity, he claimed it was led by the Antichrist himself. In such a situation, Tyrrell's moral obligations were clear. The Church would have to be destroyed in its traditional form.[1]

Tyrrell's antipathy to the Church was built on considerations which were partly positive and partly negative. On the positive side, Tyrrell was opposed to the Church not because he was anticlerical but because he wanted a different *kind* of Church. The Church of his dreams would be one that was responsive to and fashioned by the exigencies of the inner life. In the Church of his day, however, he saw little relation between interior realities and exterior structure. The *Leibkirche* was not determining the *Geistkirche*; the invisible, the visible Church; the dynamic of the People of God, the official hierarchy. The inversion of values which he saw was a scandal. He made this point in many different ways throughout his theological career, but a passage already cited is particularly clear in its analysis of the Church:

> a man might have great faith in the Church, in the people of God, in the unformulated ideas, sentiments and tendencies at work in the great body of the faithful, and constituting the Christian and Catholic 'Spirit'; and yet regard the Church's consciously formulated ideas and intentions about herself as more or less untrue to her deepest nature; that he might refuse to believe her own account of herself as against his instinctive conviction of her true character.[2]

That the hierarchy should be subservient to the interests of Christian life was also one of the themes in Tyrrell's correspondence with Bishop A.H. Mathew, leader of the Old Catholics in England. These letters frequently reveal Tyrrell's impish humor, but they can hardly conceal his growing frustration. In September, 1900, Tyrrell wrote that "Pius X tells us the Church is governed from above and not from below. He should remember that she is financed from below and that those who pay the piper will call the tune."[3] The tune Tyrrell wanted to hear was not the one being piped. Said he, "L'Eglise c'est moi is literally the Pope's attitude.

He is the steam engine; the episcopate is the carriages; the faithful are passengers."[4] The Church authorities were not responsive to the religious feelings of the whole People of God. This insensitivity was seen in the dominance of the Vatican by Italians. In a sarcastic letter to Mathew, Tyrrell said that he had addressed a "pastoral" to some Italians to agitate for a "people-elected Pope." Then he added:

> But the Pope must be an Italian or Roman so as to exclude the international idea of the Papacy; just as I always contend that *all* the Cardinals must be Italians. It is only the universal pretensions that make it unjust that the Universe should be governed by Italians.[5]

It follows from these ideas that authority in the Church should derive not from ecclesiastical status but from the content of religious experience. Tyrrell summed up this position in a letter to Mathew, saying that "the *principle* of anti-Vaticanism is that supreme authority rests with the whole Church and not with Rome..."[6] Similarly, he argued:

> One must add to these another Category of Modernism, condemned by Pius X under the name 'Laicism' and 'Presbyterianism', which consists in a protest against the progressive centralization of the Roman Church, by which first the laity, then the priests, and finally the bishops, have been deprived of all active share in Church life and government; which demands constitutional guarantees for the liberty of the subject against the caprices of authority; and which is inspired by the idea of democracy as well as by a knowledge of the original constitution of the Church. This is the most widespread of all forms of Modernism, and is shared by thousands who would cordially anathematise Dom Romolo Murri as well as M. Loisy.[7]

Imagining himself as the newly elected Pope, Tyrrell summarized his views, especially as they affected Roman centralization, in an "encyclical" sent to his friend Mathew:

> My first encyclical would remind my brethren that as all my authority derives from the *populus Romanus*, so theirs from the faithful of their dioceses; that each diocese is a *societas perfecta* and only of its own free and reversible choice federated with any other; that the bond of any bigger aggregate is free and spiritual; in no sense juridical; that Masses etc. are valid because they are the acts of a community (when 2 or 3, etc.); that 'orders' are simply delegation and can take any form the community chooses e.g. Tom, Dick, or Harry *might* be told off [*sic.*] to say Mass just for one occasion, and possess orders for half-an-hour; that orders are only indelible because and when the community so wills it.[8]

Authority in the Tyrrellian conception is spiritual rather than juridical. It derives from Christ and not from the Church. Because it derives from Christ, the center of Church life is not in Rome but in Him. The only union which is necessary is that between the local Church and its spiritual Head; there is no required union between church and church under their bishop.

It needs to be noted, however, that there is considerable ambiguity in the way that Tyrrell uses expressions such as "Spirit of Christ", "spirit of

Christ," and "Divine Spirit." There is seldom any metaphysical connotation to the term "Spirit," but more commonly it is used as a synonym for a moral or religious experience. God is known to us, not through reason's bare perusal of Him, but through His effects in the religious consciousness. Tyrrell will speak of the action whereby God engages us under the terms "Divine Spirit" or "Spirit of Christ." But he can also speak of the "spirit of Christ," by which he means Christ's human spirit as touched and transformed by God, and this term is therefore a synonym for Jesus' aims, his religious vision.

Consequently, it is possible to speak of both the "spirit of Christ" and the "Spirit of Christ." The former would be appropriate when referring to a uniformity in outlook between Christ and his Church; the latter would be appropriate when identifying the moral and religious impulses in the Church which are the results of the fresh, contemporary manifestations of God.

Tyrrell was never in any doubt that the "Spirit" needs as its vehicle of expression a physical "envelope." He was not in the least opposed to the visible Church, but he did take issue with the way it had developed, how it was structured, and the type of authoritarianism it generated.

The structure of the Church was not responsive to the manifestation of the Spirit. This condition indicated that it was animated by the Spirit of "Antichrist." Tyrrell, however, was not conventional in his use of this term. To him the term had no metaphysical connotations and was merely a synonym for that malaise and egocentricity in the Church bureaucracy by which genuine spiritual concerns were smothered. Thus he declared:

> I believe in the Roman Church so far as it is Christian and Catholic; I disbelieve in it so far as it is papal. I see two spirits in it, as in myself, struggling for supremacy — Light and Darkness, Christ and Anti-Christ; God and the Devil. At present Christ is thrown and Anti-Christ is uppermost.... I look for the day when Peter, after his boasted fidelity and manifold denials, *aliquando conversus, confirmabit fratres.* It is a long way off from that blessed cock-crow.[9]

Despite the difficulties created by nineteenth century biblical criticism, Tyrrell was not one to take refuge in the "citadel mentality." The consequences were to be faced squarely, even if the vitals of traditional Catholic faith were impugned. In this connection, he was driven to recognize that some of the most penetrating thrusts from biblical criticism had taken place at the point where the papacy was most vulnerable. Writing of the fate of the Petrine texts on which the papacy was built, he admitted:

> Criticism suspects many of these texts (especially from St. Matt.) to be interpolations in the interests of the early ambitions of Rome; or to be the reporter's vision, or perversion of Christ's words rather than the words themselves, or to be mere fabricated (though characteristic) utterances put into his mouth, after the literary custom of those times... altogether inadequate to the purposes of the apologist *pro ecclesia infallibili.*[10]

Tyrrell believed that the validity of the papal office in orthodox Catholic theology depended on the acceptability of the notion of biblical inerrancy, especially as it related to the Petrine texts. "If the latter conception has to be gravely modified," he said, "the former cannot hope to escape a corresponding modification."[11] The critical work of Gunkel, Jülicher, Holtzmann and Weiss, however, was slowly forcing Tyrrell to introduce serious modifications into both notions.

Tyrrell was not unaware of the arguments on which biblical inerrancy had been justified. But as he examined these arguments, he believed that he had detected not only some bad logic but also a lack of candor. The conclusion of the argument was assumed in the premise; the church supported biblical inerrancy on the twin pillars of fulfilled prophecy and the occurrence of miracles. In order to do so, it first had to assume that it had in its possession an inerrant account of both the prophecy and the miracles. This assumption Tyrrell could not make. Thus he wrote:

> Old Testament criticism has robbed prophecies, New Testament criticism has robbed miracles, of nearly all their apologetic value...the *consensus* of current criticism of even the more moderate sort makes the Bible an insufficient basis for the scientific establishment of a single indisputable miracle or a single clear fulfillment of prophecy.[12]

Criticism, then, had undermined belief in the authenticity of the biblical documents no less than in Christ's own prophetic infallibility. By opening up the possibility of later interpolations in the documents, it had forced the Church to abandon the notion that it possessed Christ's original utterances.

Tyrrell was certain, as Alfred Loisy was,[13] that Jesus never really intended to found a Church. Jesus had believed, mistakenly as it turned out, that the world would reach its cataclysmic termination in His own lifetime. Consequently, He made no preparation for a Church to perpetuate His work beyond His death.[14] The origins of institutional Catholicism, therefore, could not go back to the apostle Peter.[15] Instead, Tyrrell located these origins in Clement's *First Letter to the Corinthians*, customarily dated around 95 A.D.

In Tyrrell's view, the arguments which had led him to this conclusion were decisive, but the *coup de grâce* was administered along a different line. Even if it is assumed that the Church does possess the *ipsissima verba* of Christ in the Petrine texts—an unlikely assumption in Tyrrell's opinion—nonetheless these texts could not be forced to bear the construction traditional theology had placed upon them. These texts were addressed to the apostles. In the movement from apostolic authority to medieval political sovereignty, "there is a *transitus in aliud genus*; nor is there anything in the Gospels nor perhaps in the whole New Testament, which shows that the writers there directly contemplated or even foresaw this *transitus*."[16]

If the argument on which traditional ecclesiology was based was so evidently fallacious, why did the Church continue to maintain these beliefs? The prime reason, Tyrrell concluded, was that it was in its interests to do so. Traditional theologians, he observed dryly, "defend and define their authority; who are defended by it in return."[17] Consequently, he summarily dismissed the entire papal institution and in particular its infallibility in these words:

> Dictated by political expediency, inspired by papal arrogance, supported by fictions and forgeries, formulated by S. Thomas Aquinas, repudiated by the Reformers, contested by the Jansenists and Gallicans, defended and prompted by Jesuits, all but defined and imposed by the Vatican council, it still lives on in the teeth of history, in defiance of criticism, precisely on account of its alluring and fallacious simplicity.[18]

The suspicion that the papacy was a monstrous fraud agitated Tyrrell's mind for some years before his excommunication sealed these convictions. Those conciliar decisions which seemed to provide underpinning for the papacy were to Tyrrell extremely galling. In 1903, for example, he wrote bitterly that theological originality was being suppressed as a direct outcome of the view of Church authority endorsed by Vatican I. But not even the heavy hand of officialdom could hide from Tyrrell the fact that the causes of which the papacy was the product were not only very natural but were positively anti-Christian. To von Hügel, he wrote:

> I find it so hard to see any difference between the causes that have shaped Papal absolutism, the anti-Christian principles and characteristics of that absolutism, its spiritually corruptive and sterilizing influence; and the causes, nature and effects of the Czardom, or any other despotism.[19]

Tyrrell was obviously being pushed into a position of implacable opposition to the papacy. Indeed, he was quite candid about his role in the Church. His intention, as we have noted, was to destroy Catholicism as it had existed traditionally. He liked to think of himself as a new "David" plotting the downfall of "Pope Giant." "One little pebble of hard historical concrete slung into the center of the Pope's forehead is all we need," he said. But he did add, a little ruefully, "for that we need a thousand slingers hard at it."[20] Apparently the Pope learned something of these dark machinations, for in another letter Tyrrell admitted that "the Pope calls me an anti-Pope."[21] The appellation, however, seemed to delight him.

Tyrrell's candor disturbed his more conservative friends. Did the theologians not counsel dissidents to suppress their misgivings and submit to papal authority? They did indeed, Tyrrell replied, but their argument left him unmoved:

> After all, it is not Catholicism but the theology of Catholicism; not authority, but the theology of authority; not the Church but that theological school which usurps

her functions that we have to fight against. If theologians quote authority against us they beg the question for it is their whole *theory* of authority which is in question far more than any detail of authoritarian teaching.[22]

For Tyrrell to place himself under the Pope's authority again would be to return to the Antichrist's sway from which he sought deliverance. Whatever reluctance the new "David" might have had in acting out the role he had cast for himself, he was clear in his own mind where the path of duty lay. "Goliath" had to be slain. As it turned out, biblical history was not to be repeated, for it was "David" rather than "Goliath" who was decapitated!

Tyrrell's personal antipathy to Pius X was extraordinarily intense.[23] When his disconnected utterances about Pius are pieced together, it would seem that this antipathy was built on three notions which need to be read with varying degrees of seriousness. First, he doubted the Pope's sanity. Second, he was convinced that the Pope was a heretic and, third, he believed that the Pope was in schism.

References to papal insanity were reserved, understandably, for private correspondence, and they illustrate Tyrrell's large capacity for hyperbole. One reference occurs in a letter to von Hügel in which Tyrrell was complaining of disciplinary measures taken against Modernist sympathizers:

Apart from the misery of these victims of the reign of Terror one cannot but rejoice to see folly cutting its throat so thoroughly. Quite seriously I think our good Pope is not all there. The *Tablet* says that though *this* week (for a wonder) has brought no new *motu proprio* yet the Pope has told someone that he has ten more ready in his drawer. Does this not savour of insanity?[24]

Tyrrell's views on the Pope's sanity probably said more about his own frustration than the Pope's rational faculty, but the other charges which he leveled against the head of his Church need to be taken more seriously. These complaints, however, have to be seen against the backdrop of Tyrrell's own thought to which brief allusion has been made.

As we have seen, Tyrrell's theology of the Church was built on three closely related principles. First, he believed that the Church's hierarchy receives its mandate to govern not from the Pope but from the People to whom it is alone responsible. From this belief it follows, second, that the hierarchy can only teach that which accords with the substance of religious experience common to all Catholics. Authority, then, is a predicate of corporate religious experience rather than a consequence of ecclesiastical status. Third, hierarchical orders are constituted not through juridical relationship to the Pope but through sacramental union with Christ.

It is the second of these three principles in particular which really explains Tyrrell's extraordinary charge that the Pope was both heterodox and schismatic. His views on this subject were brought into the open in

December, 1900, when the English Catholic hierarchy issued its pastoral entitled "The Church and Liberal Catholicism."[25] In fact, the teaching of the pastoral was neither unusual nor unexpected, but Tyrrell thought it was positively scandalous. In the pastoral, the English bishops argued for the traditional distinction between the *Ecclesia Docens* (the teaching Church) and the *Ecclesia Discens* (the taught Church). The former, it was said, had been entrusted with both the knowledge of what constituted the faith (the *depositum fidei*) and with the responsibility of communicating it to the laity, the *Ecclesia Discens*. The latter, it was argued, had been charged with the responsibility of receiving the faith thus communicated and of obeying it.

The pastoral enfuriated Tyrrell. He veiled his anger better in his public utterances, however, than in his private ones. Publicly, he observed that those who followed authority blindly would have no difficulty in following this teaching. But it was quite unacceptable to those who, "in the light of history, distinguish between the Pope as the voice of a theological clique and the Pope as the voice of the universal Church past and present."[26] In his familiar role as the captive of a theological clique, the Pope was arrogating to himself authority which belonged to Christ alone, for it was quite evident that the whole function ascribed to the *Ecclesia Docens* had been usurped by the Pope. The dangers implicit in this crushing despotism were all too obvious. "The Pope was not less infallible in the days of Honorius than he is now, nor was less obedience due to the Arianising bishops than to those of the present day."[27]

In private, whatever temperance Tyrrell had mustered was unceremoniously abandoned. To von Hügel, the pastoral was described as

> a most preposterous and heretical document which implies a brand-new conception of the constitution of the Church. The bishops have mounted on metaphors, as witches on broomsticks, and have ridden to the devil. It is the sheep and shepherd article that does the trick. The sheep are brainless, passive; their part is to be led, fed, fleeced and slain for the profit of the shepherd for whose benefit they exist. Apply this to the constitution of the Church and where are you to stop? And then there is the Divine Teacher fallacy! Christ is God; Peter is Christ; the Pope is Peter, *ergo* he is, we dare not say God, but is Divine Teacher... In Heaven's name, one asks, why doesn't he work miracles and raise the dead? Is he really present in the Blessed Sacrament?[28]

The pastoral had provoked Tyrrell beyond endurance. Retaliation was called for, although the danger of the mission required him to take refuge in anonymity. Thus sheltered, he attacked the English bishops.

Tyrrell rejected the pastoral's teaching on the relation between the *Ecclesia Docens* and the *Ecclesia Discens*. These two bodies, he argued, do not work

> as master and scholar, two distant, though related personalities; the one simply communicative the other simply receptive; but they are co-principles of one self-teaching, self-governing organism. In this view it is the Church collectively who is

properly and immediately the Vicar of Christ and the Shepherd of the Sheep, and
the episcopate and the Holy Father only in a derived and secondary sense.[29]

A radical limitation on papal power had to be implemented immediately.
The Pope's only vocation in the Church was that of articulating the
common faith experience of the whole Church. In this activity, and only
in this activity, does the Pope fulfill his own ambition of serving the
servants of God. Apart from this relationship of service, he has no
legitimate authority.[30]

Tyrrell, then, was an eager but unorthodox proponent of collegiality.
If he dubbed his own theology "Anti-Vaticanism," he did so because he
recognized that Vatican I was the great opponent of collegiality. This
judgment was probably based on that Council's rejection of St.
Antonious' formulation of papal infallibility which stated:

> The Pope, though as an individual (*singularis*) person and acting of himself (*motu
> proprio*) can err in faith; nevertheless, using the counsel and seeking the help (*utens
> consilio et requirens adiutorium*) of the universal Church, God so ordaining, who
> said 'I have prayed for thee,' he cannot err; nor can it be that the universal Church
> should accept something as Catholic that is heretical, because the universal Church
> is the Bride, and will ever be 'without spot or wrinkle.'[31]

The final text from the Council pointedly omitted the statement that in
defining dogma the Pope should work in concert with and use the
counsel and help of the Church. According to Cuthbert Butler, many of
the Council fathers were distressed by this omission, believing that it
represented "a disuniting of head and body in the supreme matter of
defining truth, a decapitating of the Church, a decorporating of the
Pope."[32]

It is this condition of a decapitated Church and a decorporated Pope
that was at the heart of Tyrrell's twofold charge against the Pope. Traditionally, of course, schism has been defined as the departure, on the part
of a group or individual, from the main body of Catholic believers
resulting in their severance from the Pope. Like Hans Küng, however,
Tyrrell broadened his definition to include not merely an individual's
schism from the Pope but also the Pope's schism from the Christian Body.
It is perfectly conceivable, Tyrrell argued, for the Pope to detach himself
from the Body and to pursue a course of theological independence. In
this case, whatever authority he formerly had in his role as spokesman for
the whole Body has been jeopardized. When the Pope severs his relationship to the People as their servant, he is, in the nature of the case,
depriving himself of all valid authority, for such authority is derived from
the People *in toto*. Actions which are the fruit of this theological independence are not only illegitimate, but they can only be foisted on the
Church through pretense and a counterfeit authority.

Tyrrell was convinced that this broken relationship between the Pope
and his People constituted schism. It also constituted a reckless breach

of Catholic tradition and, as such, amounted to heterodoxy. Behind the "decorporating of the Pope" lay an errant theology which had reached its climax in the First Vatican Council. This theology was based on fraud and inspired by arrogance.

Tyrrell was in no doubt at all that it was the Pope's Catholicism which was in question rather than his own. To von Hügel he said:

> it is they who are in peril. At most one's fears should be that of a nurse or doctor for a violently delirious patient. But a point comes when one can do no more... Pius X and Del Val will do what we could not do—will help the fever of fanaticism to burn itself out. From the ashes a new Phoenix will rise.[33]

Tyrrell's Catholicism and the Pope's were related to each other as Light is to Darkness and as Christ is to Antichrist. Papal theorizing about the Church was deceitful, heterodox, and schismatic. By contrast, the impulses which had formed Tyrrell's convictions were rooted in "Conscience." It is far better, he said, for one to choose "the censure of fallible man to that of his Conscience."[34]

And so ended one of the more extraordinary and bizarre episodes in the history of the Catholic dissent. Yet the issues which Tyrrell raised were by no means outlandish, and at the Second Vatican Council many of his ideas were quietly adopted. That the papal office is once again under scrutiny, collegiality has been firmly endorsed by the Council, and there is in the documents of Vatican II a spiritual conception of the Church as well as juridical one means that Tyrrell cannot be brushed aside with indifference simply on the grounds that Pius X declared him to be a heretic.

The equation Tyrrell made between "Vaticanism" and a juridical and strongly papal conception of the Church is correct. The chapter titles of Vatican I's Constitution on the Church are suggestive: "Of the Institution of the Apostolic Primacy in Blessed Peter;" "On the Perpetuity of the Primacy of Blessed Peter in the Roman Pontiffs;" "On the Power and Nature of the Primacy of the Roman Pontiffs;" "Concerning the Infallible Magisterium of the Roman Pontiff." The Constitution claims that it is dealing with the whole nature of the Church of Christ, but it seems to deal only with the nature of the Pope. Tyrrell was not far off in claiming that the Pope's attitude was literally "L'Eglise c'est moi." Despite some recent, valiant efforts to see elements of collegiality in the decisions of Vatican I, Tyrrell's judgment must stand. The rejection of St. Antonius' formula and the deliberate omission of the words "using the counsel and seeking the help of the universal Church" from the text on papal infallibility leaves little room for debate on this question.

The atmosphere at Vatican II, however, was quite different. The introduction of the theme "People of God" in the second chapter of *Lumen Gentium* immediately alerts the reader to the fact that there is a conception of the Church in the documents which is spiritual and not juridical.

The best expression of this shift came a little later in this Constitution in the much celebrated teaching on collegiality.

The theory of collegiality is quite simple. Jesus chose the twelve apostles to continue his work and then, from among their number, he selected Peter as the leader.[35] Because Jesus chose Peter as leader *after* he had chosen the other apostles Peter's authority was no different from that of any other apostle.[36] In the second stage of the argument, the Council followed tradition by arguing for apostolic succession.[37] The order of bishops succeeds that of the apostles not merely because the bishops have come after the apostles but because the apostles, as it were, live on in the bishops.[38] An identity exists between them, and the result is that the episcopal office enjoys the authority of the apostolic office.[39] If the bishops have succeeded the apostles, the Pope has succeeded Peter. But Peter's authority was not different from that of any other apostle and, it follows, the Pope's authority is not really different from that of any other bishop. It is not surprising that some of the fathers feared, as Williams says, that "the Pope would become ultimately no more than a *primus inter pares*, answerable to and dependent upon the college of bishops of which he himself is a member."[40]

The fear was not to be realized, because Pope Paul VI, who had succeeded John between the first and second sessions of the Council, added to the end of the Constitution an Explanatory Note. The Council had no opportunity to vote on it. The Note allows that the Pope is part of the collegial college, but it appears to exempt from collegial action those papal actions which arise out of his role as "Vicar of Christ and shepherd of the universal Church."[41] Two kinds of papal action are still possible: the Pope may act as head of the college of bishops and the Pope may act as shepherd of the universal Church.[42] The Note even denies that there is "any *equality* between the head and the members of the college" and claims that the Pope has a right to proceed "according to his own discretion and in view of the welfare of the Church in structuring, promoting, and endorsing any exercise of collegiability."[43]

The confusion created by this Explanatory Note still awaits resolution, but it can scarcely be denied that the collegial view espoused by Tyrrell is now widely held by a majority of the bishops. They believe, as he did, that papal authority should not be used and, indeed, cannot validly function independently of the whole body of bishops.

Of course, it is true that the traditional statement on infallibility was endorsed at the Council, and at first sight this endorsement would seem to leave the Pope's powers intact. He has "full, supreme, and universal power over the Church" and he "can always exercise this power freely."[44] But progressives have sought to see even this authority as a part of the Church's functioning as a whole. Referring to the phrase "can always exercise this power freely," Butler says: "The word translated *can* is *valet*.

It appears to mean that when the Pope so acts [with consultation] his action is 'valid.' It does not, in that case, imply that the Pope is morally justified in acting without due consultation."[45]

An important corollary to the theme "People of God" and to the spiritual conception of the Church is a greater emphasis on the laity. Schillebeeckx has rightly said that in recent centuries the question has been asked as to what is the place of the laity in the Church, whereas in biblical times the question was inverted: what is the place of the clergy in the Church?[46] For the first time in conciliar history, a specific decree on the laity was issued, and for the first time a council stated that lay people have full possession of the Spirit.[47] This statement means that a limited endorsement of the priesthood of all believers has taken place.[48] The outcome might be, as Butler has suggested, that the Church as a whole might act under both its traditional roles as *docens* and *discens*.[49] The content of the *sensus fidei*, which is possessed by the whole Body and is a result of the Spirit's presence, provides the substance of what is taught, and the whole Body, insofar as it articulates what it senses and perceives, assumes the magisterium's role of teaching the substance of faith. If this is the case, then Tyrrell's contention that the whole Church has the Spirit and that it acts both as *docens* and *discens* has been conceded by the Second Vatican Council.

The encyclical *Pascendi* was critical of some of these ideas. The Modernists' theology, it said, amounted to "the introduction of that most pernicious doctrine which would make of the laity the factor of progress in the Church."[50] It went on to summarize the Modernists' argument for a more spiritual conception of the Church:

> They cry out that ecclesiastical government requires to be reformed in all its branches, but especially in its disciplinary and dogmatic departments...a share in ecclesiastical government should therefore be given to the lower ranks of the clergy, and even to the laity, and authority which is too much concentrated, should be decentralized.[51]

This doctrine was quite unacceptable. The encyclical argued that this view was simply part of the attempt to uproot the traditional Church.

It is important to see that Tyrrell's concern was far broader than the issue of papal infallibility alone. He did want this dogma to be rescinded or negated, but he also wanted a different kind of Church. What he wanted was realized in theory at the Second Vatican Council. It is in the implementation of the new ecclesiology, especially as it concerns collegiality, that problems have arisen. These problems, not surprisingly, are now largely associated with the extent and exercise of papal powers. The atmosphere in which these matters are now being discussed is very different from that which pertained sixty years ago. Hans Küng's scathing attack on papal infallibility, *Infallible? An Inquiry*, would have been unthinkable in Tyrrell's day. Though Tyrrell's rejection of traditional papal powers was as firm as Küng's, the public expression of it was considerably more muted.[52] Nevertheless, history is once again moving over the same ground, turning up the same problems, stimulating comparable responses, and leading the Church to decide once again what powers it will vest in its constitutional head. Tyrrell's answers may have appeared outlandish sixty years ago, but the issues he confronted were of vital importance to Catholic life. In the intervening decades they seem to have resisted any final resolution, which suggests that Tyrrell's ideas may not be so outlandish after all.

During the years between the demise of Modernism and the formulation of that New Catholicism which Vatican II defined and heralded, the Church has undergone a transformation of great importance. On the one hand, the scholastic orthodoxy which once reigned in the Church and which made Tyrrell's theology appear so *avant garde* has either disappeared or been rectified. On the other hand, a new form of orthodoxy has now emerged which, for its own reasons and on its own terms, is utilizing theological principles that are similar to Tyrrell's. The chasm that once divided Tyrrell's Modernism from the orthodox consensus has been closed. Tyrrell's theology, once withered by the blast of ecclesiastical censure, now appears prophetic and even seminal.

Chapter Five

SEARCHING FOR REVELATION

There are at least two major problems encountered in the idea of biblical revelation. First, what is the exact nature of the revelatory element and, second, what is its relationship to the written text? Of the two problems, it is probably the second which has proved most difficult to solve, at least in the period subsequent to the development of biblical criticism. If it can be agreed that God does in some way make a disclosure of Himself to man, does He use the written Word to mediate this disclosure? If not, does Scripture have an alternative role to play which is independent of the disclosure? The variety of theories which have sought to resolve this problem is common knowledge in theological circles. Although the range and ramifications of the discussion are outside the scope of this study, it is important to note that there are two basic approaches to the problem, both of which offer an important point of connection with Tyrrell's theology and that of Vatican II. The one approach, within which there is variety and dissent, has generally been espoused by most traditional Protestants and Roman Catholics. It has identified revelation with the written text of the Bible. The second model, adopted by Protestant Liberalism, identified revelation with religious experience. Scripture, then, became the first chapter in the long story of God's education of man. This first chapter happened to be a very important one inasmuch as it recorded apostolic experience. In a derived and secondary sense, then, the Bible was viewed as revelatory. These two approaches have usually been considered contradictory to one another, but recently there have been those who, wittingly or otherwise, have seen them as different but complementary.

Neo-orthodoxy, for example, has attempted to reconcile the two emphases by insisting, on the one hand, that God personally confronts man in the act of disclosure but, on the other, that He uses the written Word in a mediatorial role. Those who are more traditional emphasize the importance of the written Word, while those who are less traditional, like Bultmann, emphasize the first aspect, that of existential encounter. Many other variations have also been developed. There is obviously justification for saying, then, that a discussion of revelation under the rubric either of propositions or experience is a vast oversimplification.

The issue is much more complex than this. Nevertheless, it does enable one to cut through the tangled complexities of recent discussion and see the problem in its raw makings. To this limited extend, it is a useful point of departure.

The twin foci of the problem of revelation were accentuated almost accidentally by the Second Vatican Council. It was to be expected that the Council would follow tradition and identify the Divine disclosure with the written Word, and so it did. It was not expected that hints would also appear that the act of disclosure occurs independently of the biblical text in moments of religious experience. Viewed as a whole, then, the Council's teaching on revelation is not entirely consistent. The second theme, it is true, is not really developed at any great length. It would be incorrect to say that two theologies were represented in the conciliar documents; yet it would also be incorrect to say that there is only one.[1]

The Council was expected to endorse the traditional view of biblical revelation. The Council of Trent had declared its belief in the inspiration of the whole of Scripture, thereby identifying revelation with the biblical text. The scope of inspiration was apparently considered wide enough to cover both the historical and religious matters with which Scripture deals.[2] Later, the attempt at disengaging revelation from the content of the written Scripture was condemned in the Syllabus of Errors in 1864. It is erroneous to think, it was said, that divine revelation is "subject to a continual and indefinite progress which corresponds with the progress of human reason."[3] The same point was made in 1870 by the First Vatican Council. The Scriptures, "having been written by the inspiration of the Holy Ghost," the Council declared, "have God for their author...."[4] There can be no admixture of error in these inspired writings.[5] In his encyclical letter *Providentissimus Deus* of 1893, Leo XIII continued this line of thought with a long exposition on the nature of biblical revelation. These God-inspired writings are "His own oracles and words," Leo said, and he added that "to be ignorant of Scripture is not to know Christ."[6] Citing the patristic view, the encyclical affirms that the biblical documents, "in all their parts were equally from the *afflatus* of Almighty God, and that God, speaking by the sacred writers, could not set down anything which was not true."[7] Finally, this well established opinion was reasserted by Pius X in his condemnation of Modernist heresy. Responding to the Modernist view that Scripture deals with moral and religious matters, not scientific and historical ones, and therefore that it contains errors, His encyclical *Pascendi* stated:

> We, Venerable Brethren, for whom there is but one only truth, and who hold that the Sacred Books, written under the inspiration of the Holy Ghost, have God for their author (Conc. Vat., *De Revel.*, C.2) declare that this is equivalent to attributing to God himself the lie of utility or officious lie, and We say with Augustine: 'In an

authority so high, admit but one officious lie, and there will not remain a single
passage of those apparently difficult to practice or to believe, which on the same
most pernicious rule may not be explained as a lie uttered by the author wilfully
and to serve a purpose.'[8]

This statement has, of course, gone beyond the identification of
revelation with the biblical text to teach as a self-evident corollary, the
Bible's inerrancy. This corollary is not as self-evident today as it was then,
although the historical commitment which has been outlined was
honored by Vatican II in the following words:

> Since everything asserted by the inspired authors or sacred writers must be held to
> be asserted by the Holy Spirit, it follows that the books of Scripture must be
> acknowledged as teaching firmly, faithfully, and without error that truth which God
> wanted put into the sacred writings for the sake of our salvation.[9]

Some theologians have seen loopholes in the Council's teaching,
even though its grammatical structure and phraseology duplicates a section of teaching from Vatican I which had no intention of leaving
loopholes.[10] Butler, for example, has suggested that the truth which the
passage guarantees as inerrant relates only to salvation. Furthermore, he
declares that no specification has been made as to the precise nature or
limits of "that truth" which God wanted in the sacred writings.[11] Nevertheless, it does seem evident that in this passage the Council intended to
equate revelation with the biblical record.

Alongside this view, however, appeared a notion which was, to some
observers, rather unexpected. An identification was suggested between
revelation and man's experience of salvation. Writing of this theme,
Tavard has said:

> The Plan of the Constitution is not merely a matter of organization; it is mainly one
> of doctrine... revelation is neither essentially a doctrine, although it implies one; nor
> a set of propositions and formulations to be believed, although it may be partially
> expressed in such propositions.... Essentially revelation is a life. It is the very life of
> God imparted to man through the incarnation of the Son; it is the communication
> of God's Word understood by man in the Holy Spirit. Thus the first and last chapters
> of the Constitution constitute the general framework of the document and of the
> doctrine it teaches. The first explains how God reveals himself; the last shows how
> Christians may develop the life of God in themselves by better following the mind
> of God as shown in the Holy Scriptures.[12]

The unexpected theme first comes to the reader's attention in the text
chosen as a preface to the Constitution on Revelation: "We announce to
you the eternal life which was with the Father, and has appeared to us...
(1 Jn. 1:2-3)." The interconnection between God's eternal, saving life and
His revealing activity is picked up in the first article: "In His Goodness
and Wisdom, God chose to reveal Himself...Through this revelation,
therefore, the invisible God... lives among them [man] (cf. Bar. 3:38), so
that He may invite and take them into fellowship with Himself."[13] The

giving of revelation and the receiving of the Gospel are not unrelated events.[14] Indeed, since Christ is the source of both, they are experienced simultaneously. Revelation of God is inextricably a part of saving encounter with Him.

This interconnection between Divine disclosure and saving encounter harmonizes well with the new concern for a christocentric theology, which is perhaps evidence of Barth's influence on Roman Catholic thought. The historical element that is suggested by this concatenation of salvation and revelation was absent from the corresponding document of Vatican I. But at Vatican II Christ is seen to be God's mystery no less than its revealer, the object of revelation as well as the agent who brings it to man. And if He is the object of revelation, He is the means not only of its communication, but also of salvation which is the chief effect of such revelation. Revelation is essentially about salvation. A saving encounter with Christ, therefore, brings to man the substance of revelation. Summarizing this aspect of the Council's teaching, Butler has said that "a revelation is not fully given until it is received. It exists, in other words, in a revelational situation which is an interpersonal situation."[15]

The differences between propositional and experiential revelation are plain. In a propositional emphasis revelation, which is identified with the biblical text, is seen to have been delivered to man; in the more fluid emphasis on experience revelation is not really given until it has been personally received. On the one view the limits of revelation are fixed. The Church possesses it *in toto* now, although understanding of that revelation develops. On the other view the extent of revelation in Christian possession seems to vary. How much is given is dependent on how much is received and that depends on how close the Christian's relationship is to Christ. This analysis may be a little overdrawn, but the fact that there is traditional theology juxtaposed alongside a liberal view in the constitution is inescapable.

That the Council should have taught the traditional view is not surprising; that it should grant any legitimacy to the newer ideas is surprising. The encyclical letter *Pascendi* specifically rejected the idea that revelation may in any way be identified with religious experience. The encyclical states:

> Modernists find in this *sense* [religious consciousness] not only faith, but in and with faith, as they understand it, they affirm that there is also to be found revelation. For, indeed, what more is needed to constitute a revelation? Is not that religious *sense* which is perceptible in the conscience, revelation, or at least the beginning of revelation? Nay, is it not God Himself manifesting Himself, indistinctly, it is true, in this same religious *sense*, to the soul? And they add: Since God is both the object and the cause of faith, this revelation is at the same time *of* God and *from* God, that is to say, God is both the Revealer and the Revealed.[16]

The idea condemned here, that God is "the Revealed" and "the Revealer," comes very close to the notion hinted at by the Council: Christ is God's mystery and the revealer of God's mystery, the object of revelation no less than the agent through which it comes to man.

The importance of these two approaches to revelation becomes clear when attention is shifted back to Tyrrell's thinking on this matter. His ideas were not entirely representative of Modernist theology in general. Indeed, subsequent to the early months of 1907, he held to a balance of traditional and progressive ideas that is a remarkable anticipation of the decision arrived at by the Council. When *Pascendi* berated Modernists for holding the view that revelation is only given in experience, it was condemning a view that had at one time been held by Tyrrell but that he himself had modified just prior to the publication of the encyclical. A measure of injustice was perpetrated by the encyclical, but, of course, this was inevitable if thinkers of widely different interests and sometimes ideas should be condemned in a single document.

In order to grasp the significance of Tyrrell's position in the years after 1907, it is necessary to trace the changes and modifications in his theology of revelation prior to this time. In this connection, two distinct periods are discernible. First, from his first writings in 1866 until November, 1899, the date which separates the traditional from the progressive Tyrrell, he evidently identified revelation with the biblical text. In the second period, beginning in November, 1899, he began moving toward the liberal identification of revelation with religious experience. This movement was particularly evident in the period between January, 1904, and the closing months of 1906. Just prior to his condemnation in 1907, however, he again changed his position and attempted to forge a compromise between the two theories of revelation.[17]

It was toward the end of Tyrrell's traditionalist period that his views on revelation and dogma became evident.[18] The Divine disclosure, he said, resulted in a supernatural instruction of the human mind, "similar to the informing of one mind by another."[19] He was in no doubt as to the fact or the meaning of biblical inspiration. In view of God's revelatory activity in Scripture, the Christian repudiates the futile attempt of instructing himself about God and the world and instead allows God's revelation to do this for him. Tyrrell would not allow the traditional conception to be compromised, although he allowed for the accepted notion of development.[20] He sharply rejected Sabatier's views on this matter. It was ridiculous to claim, he argued, that "the vital germ" or "inward experiences of Christ" can be distilled from the literary forms in Scripture. The Church "treasures the original mind-forms and language in which Divine truth has been communicated to her, as it were the perishable earthen vessel in which a priceless gift is contained."[21] Referring to the biblical writings, he said that there is "no room for modification or re-utterance."[22] The Church can neither add one iota to the biblical *depositum* nor subtract one iota from it.

It follows from this conception that development pertains to the Church's understanding, not to the substance of revelation, which is fixed. This view agrees with the formula endorsed by the Council of Florence: development is a matter only of explication and application of the biblical revelation. "In these matters," Tyrrell said, "the progress is one of analysis; a mere unfolding or evolution; in no strict sense a development like that of an acorn into an oak."[23]

Once biblical revelation and the limits of development have been established in this way, the role of dogma becomes evident. As the truth is assimilated in the mind of the Church, dogmatic formulae result. Their purpose is to protect "revealed truths from the innumerable misunderstandings to which they are exposed."[24] Pursuing this idea, Tyrrell said that the Church regards dogma

> as being of divine authority—differing from the Scriptural expression only in this, that in revelation the language, though human, is divinely chosen and inspired; in dogma it is chosen by human labour and only guaranteed from error through the intervention of Providence acting, not miraculously but according to established laws.[25]

The development of dogma, then, "finds its place in those applications of revealed truth which are matters of Catholic doctrine rather than of divine faith."[26]

Despite the outward assurance with which Tyrrell had written on these themes, he was beginning to suffer from some inward misgivings about these ideas. Jean Rivière, in his classic study on Modernism, perceived this change, too:

> The conviction had formed in him, little by little, that what most needed to be done was to combat the accepted forms of religious philosophy and theology—bogged down as they were in an obsolete dogmatism which he felt certain was responsible for the confusion in understanding—and to re-establish Christian faith on the base of inner experience and, in view of modern needs, to reinterpret it in terms of life.[27]

The first visible indication of Tyrrell's shifting interests was his essay "The Relation of Theology to Devotion." He remarked some years after its publication that it was the turning point in his theological career. Similarly, his close friend Maude Petre said that it was "the keynote of his ulterior development."[28] Published in November of 1899, it divides Tyrrell the traditionalist from Tyrrell the progressive.

In this essay, Tyrrell aired his doubts about his former convictions. He then developed a line of thought which was to dominate all his subsequent writings on this theme. There is a distinction to be made between revelation and theology. Revelation concerns the presence of God in man's experience, whereas theology is the after-reflection on the experience, the intellectual explanation which follows it. This distinction is important, first, because it denies that revelation is an instruction of the mind, as Tyrrell had formerly held. In the new view, the mind has

been disengaged and separated from the act of revelation. It is important, second, because revelation has been identified with religious
experience rather than with the biblical propositions. This point emerged
in the essay when Tyrrell dealt with the idea of a *depositum fidei* which
had always been identified with biblical revelation, the "form of sound
words." Said Tyrrell:

> by the 'deposit of faith' we do not mean any primitive document, nor yet that
> expression which the faith received in the mind of its first hearers, nor yet the
> present-day expression of the faith in which that former expression is at once lost
> and preserved as the child in the man; but rather, those truths and realities which
> were expressed and seen less perfectly in earlier forms, more perfectly in later—as
> though viewed through an ever clearer and more transparent medium.[29]

The one thing that can be said with certainty of Tyrrell's thought at
this moment is that it is unclear and unsettled. What precisely constituted the *depositium* did not really emerge from the essay. But it was
evident that Tyrrell had started moving in a new direction. Revelation
was identified with experience, not with propositions, "so that both the
sayer and what is said are always the same."[30] When he carried the
argument further at a later date, Tyrrell was ready to say:

> There is no honest escape from the embarrassment but in giving up the crude notion
> of Biblical revelation altogether, and in finding the inspired element, not in the mat-
> ter dealt with, but in the mode of dealing; in the tendency not in the point attained,
> in the spirit of the artist, not in the rough fragmentary work itself. Just in the same
> way, the attempt to hold the crude notion of ecclesiastical inerrancy by a dishonest
> doctoring of formulae must be abandoned, and a wider notion frankly adopted.[31]

By 1903, Tyrrell had traveled far enough down this road that he was
able to see a development not only in the Church's theological
understanding but in the substance of revelation itself. This view, of
course, had previously been declared heretical not only by Tyrrell
himself but also by the Council of Florence. Tyrrell could not believe,
however, that the deposit of "sound words" had really been conveyed to
St. Linus and thence to the episcopal successors. This view, he said, was
nothing but a figment of the authoritarian imagination.[32] Some other
definition of the meaning of revelation had to be found.

Tyrrell sought this definition through an analysis of man's growing
experience, but he did seek to protect this revelation from human distortion. In one of three essays which appeared early in this period in his
thought, Tyrrell said that secular experience "can have no place in regard
to those truths of faith that are known and knowable solely by
revelation."[33] But even if he carefully distinguished sacred revelation and
secular experience, he could not agree with the conservatives that revelation was to be found only in Scripture, not in experience. Thus he wrote:

> It grows daily more evident that the 'explication' theory is preposterously in-
> adequate; that it can be shown step by step how the several dogmas and institutions
> have taken their present shape through the action of quite natural influences.[34]

Towards the end of 1903, it was obvious that Tyrrell had detached himself completely from his former conservatism. Although he had adopted some of the liberal ideas, he had not yet committed himself to that position without reserve. There were problems in the new stance for which Tyrrell as yet had no answers. Consequently, in January, 1904, he reviewed Wilfrid Ward's *Problems and Persons* in an article entitled "Semper Eadem I." This was an exercise intended almost wholly for Tyrrell's own edification; the readers were incidental to the plan. Sometimes the act of setting down a problem in written form aids the writer in clarifying his own mind about it. Apparently this was Tyrrell's intention in writing the review. He was sufficiently pleased with the result to allow its publication. This review was actually more like a critical essay; Ward's book provided only a useful point of departure. What Tyrrell did was to set out, in seemingly objective fashion, the scholastic and the Newmanite views on the problem of dogmatic development. Between the two positions, Tyrrell then concluded, there could be no *via media*. In his private correspondence, however, he declared that he had decided to opt for Newman's view and to follow it to its logical and liberal conclusions, an intention not made plain in the essay. The noncommittal tone in the essay later proved to be an embarrassment to him, for shortly after the essay appeared in print some conservatives, imagining that they perceived the homeward journey of the prodigal, fell over themselves to congratulate him and welcome him back into the fold! "I think I over-did my January article," he said ruefully to A.L. Lilley, "and have had congratulations from such disgusting sources that I have determined to execute an adroit climb-down in February—only the *Month* will not be so open to my liberal explanation as it was to my apparently reactionary statement."[35]

The climb-down was not received with any enthusiasm, as Tyrrell had predicted. In fact, the editor of *Month* refused to publish it. According to Tyrrell, this article was only an attempt at making explicit what had been implicit in the first essay. In his favor, it must be said that he still did not identify himself wholly with liberalism in this essay, although there is no question about where his sympathies lay.

Despite determination and high resolve, Tyrrell could find no permanent satisfaction with his theology. As the year 1907 began, he once again executed an adroit change in direction, drawing back from the liberalism to which he had been attracted. The most important change in his thinking concerned revelation. In the three years prior to this time he had come more and more to view revelation as capable of enlargement and development. In 1907, he flatly contradicted this position, saying that the was returning "to the earlier and stricter view as to the unchanging, unprogressive character of the apostolic revelation."[36] His new position, he said, was a "repudiation of all attempts to mitigate the supposed difficulties of this severer view by theories of development, dialectical or otherwise."[37] Development in theology there is, but development in revelation is impossible. Revelation is no more capable of development than is Christ, and He cannot develop.[38] Biblical revelation, therefore, "is alone normative and authoritative for Christianity...."[39] Summarizing his new position in a remarkably lucid way, Tyrrell said:

> All subsequent reflection has deepened my conviction that the liberation of the tangled interests of faith and reason, and the establishment of helpful relations between them, depend above all on fidelity to the patristic idea of the Apostolic Revelation as the authentic and normative expression of the Spirit of Christ; on the realization of the essentially prophetic and non-theological character of that more or less imaginative reconstruction of the super-natural order destined to guide the Christian heart; on the recognition that from the nature of things this revelation does not need, and is not susceptible of, development any more than is sanctity; that God our Father; Christ crucified and risen; the Holy Spirit; etc., are identical values for all times and capacities—'the same yesterday, today, and forever': that the theological and scientific categories woven into the substance of this inspired presentment are divinely sanctioned, not as theological, but only as illustrative values; that this revelation, viewed as experience, is rightly and profitably made the subject-matter of theological reflection, and that such theology, like any other science, must develop itself freely under no other limitations than those imposed by its subject-matter and the laws of thought; that the Church's teaching-office is simply to guard the Apostolic Revelation identically for all ages and capacities; that consequently her dogmatic decisions possess a protective but not a scientific or philosophical infallibility.[40]

In these words, Tyrrell sought to steer between the Scylla of liberalism and the Charybdis of scholasticism, between religion de l'Esprit and religion d'autorité. On the one hand, by arguing that the Bible is revelatory only in terms of its inward "soul," not in terms of the outward, literary "body," Tyrrell allowed biblical critics the latitude which has been denied to them by traditional Roman Catholics. On the other hand, by insisting on the finality of biblical revelation, he was providing an element of theological stability which he felt liberalism had lacked.

If Tyrrell's position was more traditional than it had been formerly, it obviously was not wholly traditional. His contention that biblical revelation is final was not a tacit endorsement of propositional revelation. Quite the reverse is the case, for even in the post-1907 period he was sharply critical of the traditional view of biblical inspiration.[41]

For Tyrrell, even in this final phase of his development, Jesus was still viewed as a prophet, one who had clothed His vision in the faltering and fallible words of man. "If He has assumed the form, why not the fallibility of men?"[42] It is true that Jesus gave a literal significance to the symbols He employed, but His words can no longer be taken at face value. Said the former Jesuit theologian:

> For Jesus, what we call His apocalyptic 'imagery' was no mere imagery but literal fact. But for us it can be so no longer. We can no longer believe in the little local heaven above the flat earth, from which Jesus is to appear in the clouds; nor in all the details of the vision governed by this conception.[43]

Yet, despite this almost Bultmannian view, Tyrrell insisted that the Bible's "form of sound words" be retained and made determinative for all theological work. It had been the error of liberalism to pass over biblical teaching, he said. But with what is it to be replaced? Man does not know enough about the Divine reality to which Scripture points to be able to build a life-view on a base other than that of Scripture. Besides, God has sanctioned the use of the biblical Word in the Church, and this sanction means that even if the Bible contains deficiences, it is adequate for the purpose for which He designed it. The teaching of Scripture, therefore, "is classical and normative for all subsequent interpretation."[44]

In view of this decision to return to the idea that revelation does not develop, it is important to note that Tyrrell, even after 1907, held the alternative view that religious experience is revelational. "It reveals God," he said, "as every cause is revealed in and with its effects; it reveals Him not in a statement but in the moral and religious impulse that proceeds from Him."[45]

It should be said that there are certain tensions evident in Tyrrell's thought which were not yet resolved. It is contradictory, for example, to insist that revelation has ceased in the apostolic period, on the one hand, and that it continues through religious experience, on the other. How can revelation have ceased and yet continue? Furthermore, can the many important images used by Jesus be discarded if at the same time they constitute revelation which is "classical" and "normative?" If God has sanctioned images which are culturally determined and erroneous, is it to be concluded that He has sanctioned what is obsolete and passé? And is man forced to believe what is erroneous simply because in his relativity he has no alternative source of truth available to him? Whether Tyrrell could have provided answers to these questions had he had the opportunity is an open question. But in this same year, 1907, the axe fell on the Modernist movement. Its leaders were excommunicated, the Church was purged, and Tyrrell shortly afterwards died.

It is intriguing to note, however, that elements of both models of revelation were retained in the final phase of Tyrrell's thought, just as they were to appear half a century later in the documents of Vatican II. In both cases, revelation was identified with the biblical text no less than with religious experience. Tyrrell equated revelation more clearly with experience and less clearly with the Scriptures, whereas at Vatican II revelation was more obviously correlated with the written Word and less so with experience.

This comparison between conciliar and Tyrrellian theology can be challenged at two points. It can be argued either that Tyrrell did not endorse propositional revelation as Vatican II did or that Vatican II did not teach the view that experience is revelational as Tyrrell did. If either point can be established, the comparison has been seriously damaged.

The argument so far has not established that there is a precise correspondence between the positions. It could not do so without falsifying the facts. All that it needs to establish is that on the theme of revelation Tyrrell's final position was less heterodox than the account of it in *Pascendi* would suggest and that, in fact, his ideas were almost duplicated by the Council. Supporting evidence for this conclusion can be found, not in some undisclosed intention on Tyrrell's part to endorse propositional revelation, but in a tacit agreement by the Council fathers to regard experience as revelational. This evidence emerges, not from the discussion on revelation itself, but from that on tradition.

The way in which revelation is conceived, be it propositionally or experientially, will determine the way in which tradition is viewed. If revelation is given experientially as God unites men to Himself, then tradition will be seen as the epistemological residue or accumulation of this encounter evident throughout the whole People of God. If revelation is identified with the propositional form of Scripture, then this body of truth will generate tradition as it is handed down from one episcopal generation to the other. In the first conception, revelation and tradition are almost identical; in the second, they are sharply distinguished. In the first view the magisterium has little part to play, whereas in the second it has a large and exclusive part to play. The work of transmitting tradition from generation to generation is done by God on the first view but by man on the second. The contention at this point is that it was the first view of tradition which triumphed at Vatican II, and with it triumphed the conception of revelation as experience.

It was, as a matter of fact, the second view which was first proposed in the draft constitution on revelation which came before the Council in November, 1962. The draft was entitled *De Fontibus Revelationis*. It taught in strong, unambiguous language that God has communicated propositionally to man in the Scriptures and, as was to be expected, it proposed a separation between Scripture and tradition. The former has already been given in full; the latter is to be channeled through the magisterium, whose God-given role it is to protect the truths of Scripture. For a few years prior to this draft, there had been some discussion about whether the polarization between Scripture and tradition was what the Council of Trent had intended, for it was on the authority of this Council that the traditional practice had been developed. But this was not the main reason for the concern which *De Fontibus* caused in the Council chambers. More important than this was the feeling that, in the past, tradition had been separated from Scripture too sharply and, what was worse, had been dominated by the magisterium. The magisterium had often identified tradition with its own views and propagated these as if they were Divinely sanctioned! As the debate proceeded, the problem of tradition was resolved by use of the first revelational model. This decision is evident both in the Council's desire to reunite Scripture and tradition and in its effort to deny control of tradition by the magisterium. On both of these points, the Council reiterated precisely the views held earlier by Tyrrell and, it seems clear, it did so for the same reason.

The first correction to the traditional view is seen in the following passage where Scripture and tradition are, after centuries of separation, reunited:

> there exists a close connection and communication between sacred tradition and sacred Scripture. For both of them, flowing from the same divine wellspring, in a certain way merge into a unity and tend toward the same end. For sacred Scripture is the word of God inasmuch as it is consigned to writing under the inspiration of the divine Spirit. To the successors of the apostles sacred tradition hands on in its full purity God's word which was entrusted to the apostles by Christ the Lord and the Holy Spirit... it is not from sacred Scripture alone that the Church draws her certainty about everything which has been revealed. Therefore both sacred tradition and sacred scripture are to be accepted and venerated with the same sense of devotion and reverence.[46]

According to this passage, there is only one source of revelation. Scripture and tradition coinhere in it but are subservient and ministrant to it. Neither Scripture nor tradition is sufficient; the Church needs both because it needs God's full revelation.[47] Neither source can be pitted against the other. Their essential harmony is guaranteed by the single revelation in which they are rooted.

The second correction to the traditional line of thought concerned the relationship between tradition and the magisterium. The suspicion that the magisterium sometimes "creates" tradition for its own purposes should be laid to rest for the future. Only that tradition already extant in Church life can be handed on by the teaching body. The Council's statement on this reads as follows: "This teaching office is not above the word of God, but serves it *teaching only what has been handed on* [my italics]."[48] Furthermore, the Council detached the tradition from the magisterium's exclusive control. Using what had been one of Tyrrell's favorite themes, it argued that all the People, and not merely the magisterium, have access to revelation and therefore can discern tradition. The Council thus argued:

> The body of the faithful as a whole, anointed as they are by the Holy One (cf: Jn. 2:20, 27), *cannot err in matters of belief* [my italics]. Thanks to a supernatural sense of faith which characterizes the People as a whole, it manifests this unerring quality when, 'from the bishops down to the last member of laity,' it shows universal agreement in matters of faith and morals... It [the People of God] clings without fail to the faith once delivered to the saints (cf: Jude 3), penetrates it more deeply by accurate insights, and applies it more thoroughly to life. All this it does under the lead of a sacred teaching authority to which it loyally defers.[49]

The Council's teaching on tradition is vague in some respects and apparently deliberately so. No distinction is made, for example, between the transmission of biblical and ecclesiastical tradition, between tradition in the apostolic period and that in the post-apostolic period. But the

Council has drawn attention to the new structure of ideas which it proposed. In this teaching, the vital distinction is that between the wellspring (revelation) and its derivatives (Scripture and tradition) or its functionaries (the magisterium and the People of God). This proposal is remarkably close to that of Tyrrell in his final phase. In the post-1907 period, he was at pains to stress the preeminence of revelation. This, he argued, is antecedent to Scripture and tradition which are its derivatives. Revelation is also antecedent to the People and magisterium, who are its servants.

If, as we have seen, the Council confronted the problem of the magisterium's relation to tradition, so did Tyrrell. His opponent was Cardinal Mercier, who argued that the substance of faith, the *depositum*, was the exclusive possession of the episcopal body. Consequently, "it is only the episcopate united with the Pope that has the right to interpret revelation officially."[50]

In Mercier's conception, the identification between tradition and the magisterium seemed inescapable. Tyrrell, however, feared, as progessives do today, that such a conception would encourage the magisterium to assume that its views were those of tradition and therefore should be propagated as if they had received divine approval. Responding to Mercier's argument, Tyrrell retorted: "I should have thought that Tradition was the process of transmission or else the thing transmitted, and not the organ of transmission."[51] Expanding this contention, he went on to say:

> If you mean that it is their [the episcopate's] office to gather up, formulate, and proclaim the sacred tradition which lives in the collective conscience of the whole Church *Discens* and *Docens*, lay and cleric, it is what every true Catholic holds. If you mean that the tradition lives exclusively in the collective episcopal conscience, or still worse (as you undoubtedly mean) in the single conscience of the Pope, your meaning is repudiated by all the churches of the East and was vehemently disputed in the West 'till, in 1870, it was apparently but not really approved by the Vatican Council. If you are right, the whole Church was in error about her essential constitution for many centuries of her existence.[52]

For Tyrrell, then, the magisterium has no autonomy or authority in respect to tradition. It cannot dominate, let alone create, tradition. Indeed, the magisterium does not even have exclusive access to it; the whole People of God has the responsibility of analyzing and penetrating sacred tradition. The magisterium's role in relation to both tradition and the People is one of service only. The task of these official teachers is merely to summarize the collective view of the whole Body, insofar as tradition has entered and informed its mind.

The parallel between Tyrrell's thought and that of Vatican II on this question of tradition is remarkable. It can be explained, it would seem, only by a mutual acceptance of the view that religious experience is revelational. It is this view which, in both cases, led to a restructuring of the problem whereby revelation was made antecedent to both Scripture and tradition. Once the content of revelation has been freed from an exclusive identification with Scripture, then it is possible to speak of finding revelation in the tradition which lives in the collective conscience of the whole Church. Tyrrell articulated this view and Vatican II did so, too, when it spoke of the unerring quality which the whole Church possesses as it penetrates "the faith once delivered to the saints" in the possession of all. The Council did say that this searching and analysis by the People of God does occur under the leadership of the magisterium. But Tyrrell, too, saw a role of leadership by the magisterium. On the crucial question as to whether the magisterium alone has access to and control of tradition, Tyrrell and Vatican II were in complete agreement— it does not.

The Council's teaching on revelation, tradition, and the magisterium has left some problems unresolved. The most important of these is the way in which some of the passages in *Pascendi* should be understood. For example, the encyclical berated the Modernists for denying that the magisterium has a self-contained authority. To argue that the Church's official teachers were merely servants of the whole Body (as Tyrrell and later Vatican II contended) would, it concluded, undo the Church. The analysis which lies behind this conclusion emerges quite clearly in the following passage from the encyclical:

> society, they say, can be a real unit unless the religious conscience of its members be one, and also the formula which they adopt. But this double unity requires a kind of common mind whose office is to find and determine the formula that corresponds best with the common conscience; and it must have, moreover, an authority sufficient to enable it to impose on the community the formula which has been decided upon. From the combination and, as it were, fusion of these two elements, the common mind which draws up the formula and the authority which imposes it, arises, according to the Modernists, the notion of the ecclesiastical magisterium. And, as this magisterium springs, in its last analysis, from the individual consciences and possesses its mandate of public utility for their benefit, it necessarily follows that the ecclesiastical magisterium must be dependent upon them, and should therefore be made to bow to popular ideals.[53]

The crisis in authority at the turn of the century was attributed by *Pascendi* to the Modernist's view of the magisterium. Because of this conception, it said, the Modernist proclaimed "his profound respect for authority, while never ceasing to follow his own judgment."[54] That the magisterium has less authority today, following the teaching of Vatican II, than it did formerly is beyond question. Similarly, there are today many Roman Catholics of whom it can also be said that they express profound respect for authority, yet never cease to follow their own judgment. Some theologians have argued that this development holds out the only genuine hope for Church renewal. Others have countered that this attitude is dangerous and that it contains all the potential for destruction of genuine Catholicism. Whatever the truth is, the historical antecedent of the present crisis is clear. Evaluations of the current situation are debatable; the parallel to Modernism no longer is.

Chapter Six

THE UNSUNG PROPHET

It is not surprising that George Tyrrell's theology proved unacceptable to the Church. As one of the chief figures in the worst Church conflict since the time of the Reformation, Tyrrell found himself constantly working in a hostile climate. This environment was not improved by Tyrrell's intemperate and recalcitrant attitude toward those in authority in the Church. His condemnation could have been predicted years before it came; he himself was always aware that he was skating on thin ice.

Some interesting questions about the nature of his condemnation have, however, arisen in recent years, given the affinities that exist between many of his ideas and those endorsed by the Second Vatican Council. Were the authorities angered by what he did as much as by what he thought? If so, might it be possible to separate his seeming heterodoxy from an acknowledged heteropraxy? And if so, could this solution explain how the Second Vatican Council joyfully affirmed what Pope Pius X so sorrowfully repudiated as the quintessence of all heresy only seventy years ago?

That this might be a fruitful line to explore is suggested by the fact that von Hügel shared many of Tyrrell's notions, was deeply immersed in the Modernist movement, and yet escaped condemnation. Is the explanation simply that he, unlike Tyrrell, acted with tact and a willingness to submit to the Church even where, in his best judgment, it was wrong in what it was doing?

At first, this comparison does not throw as much light on Tyrrell's case as it seems to promise, for there is considerable confusion over what the Baron's actual role in the movement was. The first two major studies on Modernism that appeared set the parameters for this discussion. Vidler's *The Modernist Movement in the Roman Church* hardly mentioned von Hügel at all and assigned no importance to him in the movement. Many years later, however, Vidler allowed that Maude Petre's observation is correct; there is a "gap" in the story, and as a result the "pervasive and persistent influence of the Baron" is not felt in Vidler's account of Modernism.[1] On the other hand, in *Le modernisme dans L'église* Rivière assumed that von Hügel was the hidden instigator behind every intellectual revolt in the Church at this time! Perhaps, as Loisy believed, Rivière's book was designed less to portray the movement accurately than to advance the outlook of Batiffol whose pupil Rivière had been, but it did establish one of the more invincible perceptions of the movement. The question as to whether the Baron was or was not a Modernist obviously needs further reflection.

It was this question that Lawrence Barmann set out to address in 1972 in *Baron Friedrick von Hügel and the Modernist Crisis in England*. He hoped that the ambiguous and confused situation could be resolved "once and for all." Barmann's book is a meticulous and thorough analysis, but as Thomas Loome has countered, it is unlikely that Barmann's solution will put to rest the perplexities.[2]

Within the boundaries set by Rivière and Vidler, there have been three main schools of interpreters. First, there have been those such as Joseph Fenton who have followed Rivière and have felt the Baron to be fully culpable for holding heretical views. They regret only that he succeeded, by one means or another, in eluding justice. Second, there were those at the time of the Modernist movement, such as Miss Petre and Loisy, who implicated von Hügel, not because of an inquisitional mentality such as Fenton's, but because they knew him to be one of their own. Indeed, they were doubly disappointed with him, first, for managing not to appear a Modernist and, second, for modifying his views a little later so he began to cease being one. The third school, which it was Barmann's particular design to overthrow, includes most of von Hügel's biographers, who by and large have sought to minimize his involvement in the movement. Bernard Holland, who edited his letters, has admitted that he only included those which set the Baron in a more orthodox light. In the various biographies that have been produced, two considerations have unfailingly been advanced. First, it has been pointed out that the concerns of the Modernists were just an aspect in von Hügel's much larger life which, as Vidler recently put it, included his activities as a "religious philosopher, as an authority on mysticism, as a guide of souls, and as a great Christian character."[3] Second, his subsequent development as a thinker is accented so that his Modernist phase can be diminished in its importance. Barmann met this interpretive tradition head-on. He refused to allow the "Modernist" von Hügel to recede from view. Von Hügel's connections with the movement were explicated in detail, and although Barmann despises the more conservatively minded like Fenton, he presented the Baron as inextricably and impenitently a part of the Modernist movement. And this relationship Barmann saw as that which constituted von Hügel's greatness. If Barmann is correct, and if the Church was willing, under certain circumstances, to allow a latitude of thought such as the Baron exhibited, then it may be possible to draw a line from von Hügel to those at the Second Vatican Council who similarly burst through the old restraints and forged a new outlook.

This line, however, must also pass through Tyrrell, because von Hügel's affinity for Tyrrell's thought, his endorsement of most of Tyrrell's ideas, has not and cannot be disputed. Together, for example, they agreed to adopt for their respective theologies a philosophy of "action" involving the united operation of the whole self. Undergirding this philosophy of "action," both agreed, was the hidden *élan* of God. Both adhered to a form of empiricism; both held similar views on miracles, dogma, and the nature of Scripture; both agreed that God's revelation in the religious consciousness is experienced by all people; and finally, they were united in their critical view of the Church's intellectual narrowness, its methodology, its fear of biblical and historical criticism, its refusal to take cognizance of the laity's spiritual experience, and its deep, unchecked corruption.

Surprisingly, von Hügel did not hesitate to make known his feelings about and disagreements with the Church. First of all, having chaffed against the intellectual narrowness and aridity of the ruling Scholasticism, he made it plain that he could not accept the view that Rome has an exclusive preserve on the truth. In the post-Tridentine era, this view had been strengthened by a rigid doctrine of the Church. Since there is no truth outside of Him who is the Truth incarnate, it was argued, so there can be no truth outside of the Church, which is the logical continuation of the Incarnation. Since von Hügel was convinced that the thirst for and the awareness of the Infinite were universal experiences, scholastics who limited genuine religious experience to those in the Church were living in blinkers. In repudiating this intolerance, von Hügel claimed to be following Cardinal Newman. Moreover, von Hügel's impatience with Rome's intellectual narrowness was evident in his earnest desire for liberty in biblical scholarship. His joint work with Charles Briggs, for example, showed the extent to which he believed the Church was out of accord with the assured results of criticism.[4] It shows, too, the lengths to which he was prepared to take his protest against the limitations of scholarly endeavor by dogmatic shackles. Von Hügel also believed that Church officials had espoused a narrow and unworkable theological methodology, and he did not hesitate to make his feelings known here either. The official Catholic methodology, he said, was derived from the Greco-Roman races. It was primarily deductive, discursive, and abstract, emphasizing the rational faculty to the virtual exclusion of the volitional and emotive. While this methodology was being stubbornly maintained, "the races which now lead in thought are generally addicted to apprehending Reality as concrete and organic, and by means of Intuition during or after practical Action and Experience."[5]

Second, von Hügel assailed the Church for her view of authority. The three factors of genuine religion—the institutional, the intellectual, and the mystical—had not been equally emphasized by the Church. Those in

authority had given the first element such prominence in their conception of ecclesiastical life that the other two factors had been
overshadowed and obscured. With their emphasis on the institutional,
scholastics had come to value the Pope's monarchical powers far more
than the contributions which the Church as a whole could make to its
own life and thought. The spiritual experience of the few was dominating
and excluding that of the many. "For von Hügel," said Emrich, "the complete domination of a hierarchy is precisely uncatholic as the complete
absence of an institution and its officers."[6] Church authorities, the
ecclesia docens, and those under authority, the *ecclesia discens*, should
be mutually dependent, the teaching offered by the one should be
counterbalanced by the religious experience offered by the other.[7] This
had been one of the insights of Liberal theology which both Tyrrell and
von Hügel adopted without hesitation.

Third, von Hügel, like Tyrrell, inveighed against the Church for its
worldly political ambitions. The Church desired to exercise political
power on the grounds that God is sovereign over the totality of human
life and so no part of it can exist independent of His control; hence no
part of it, political institutions included, should exist independent of the
Church's control either. Von Hügel did not question this argument, but
he could not sanction the manner in which the Church had sought to control national life. Deceitful political maneuvering, underhanded plots,
and the ruthless application of force were not consistent with a Christian
profession. Furthermore, in von Hügel's opinion, the Church was seeking
political power as an end in itself rather than as a means of uniting the
temporal world with the life of eternity. The Pope, von Hügel chided,
should be the servant of the servants of God, not the king over the kings
of the earth. Summarizing von Hügel's convictions on this matter, Emrich
said:

> Rome has often played the role of an oppressor and, in seeking temporal power for
> herself and in allying herself with those in authority, she becomes a spiritual facade
> which hides feebly the shabbyness and rottenness of decaying political and
> economic systems.[8]

Predictably, the antidotes von Hügel urged on his contemporaries were
humility and a greater concern for godly conduct both inside the Church
and out.

There were, however, differences between von Hügel and Tyrrell
which need to be noted. First of all, in ecclesiology, it is evident that von
Hügel valued the institutional element of religion more highly than did
Tyrrell. As time passed and as von Hügel's appreciation for the value of
the social cultus deepened, a clear divergence of opinion developed
between them. Tyrrell, more mystical by nature than von Hügel, only
grudgingly acknowledged the necessity of the institutional, and unlike
von Hügel he did not believe that only the Roman Catholic Church could

fulfill this need in Christian life. Von Hügel felt that leaving the Roman Catholic Church was tantamount to betrayal, whereas Tyrrell, with his looser and more tenuous relationship to Rome, was prepared to consider such a step when he felt that circumstances justified it. When it became known that Tyrrell was toying with the idea of joining the Old Catholics or even the Church of England, von Hügel became agitated and most distressed. Tyrrell scorned von Hügel's apprehension. He could not accept von Hügel's view, he said, that the only choice before him was to remain a Roman Catholic or become an agnostic. Tyrrell's reckless and, in von Hügel's view, irresponsible attitude to the Church was not compatible with Christian faith (as von Hügel understood it). It was this important difference which explained von Hügel's response to Tyrrell's two articles in *The Times*: "I am deeply grateful and touched for and by that noble bit, in the second article, about your being and remaining a Catholic, whatever may happen."[9]

There was a second difference which became obvious. In later years, von Hügel slowly moved away from the type of Modernist interpretation that Tyrrell had given to realities such as heaven, hell, and the *parousia*. The change came rather late in the Modernist story, and those looking for Modernists to condemn could have been pardoned had they missed the Baron's subtle shifting of position, which actually began before the official condemnation of the movement.

In December, 1899, the Baron commended Tyrrell's new book, *Hard Sayings*, in these words:

> And quite as dear to me, and as important, is the teaching as to the immanence of God, Heaven and Hell in each soul.... This also is a point I have so long cared for, and which so many of ours apprehend but timidly and fitfully, to say the least.[10]

The inclusion of the teaching on heaven and hell among those truths to be dealt with symbolically goes far outside the bounds of orthodoxy. It is one thing to say that God is immanent in the world and quite another to say that the words heaven and hell are descriptive of a soul's health or malfunctioning. At this point, von Hügel had clearly identified himself with the views of the Modernists. The change which his thought underwent, however, is thrown into sharp relief when the above excerpt is compared with one taken from another letter to Tyrrell written eight years later in May, 1907:

> But I felt strongly, somehow, that your treatment of the old transcendent conception of God as requiring to be reformulated, *en toutes pièces*, by an immanental one, is somehow a bit of most tempting, yet nevertheless impoverishing, simplification. God is certainly not, in any degree or sense, simply (spatially) outside of, or above, us; and these spatial pictures have indeed all to be interpreted in terms of spiritual experience and reality. But this experience itself is essentially as truly of God transcendent as of God immanent; of a Spirit infinitely more spiritual, a reality which is nobler and of a higher nature than our highest, and leaves us with a noble thirst—as well as of this same Spirit as penetrating us through and through, and as

satisfying our cravings. If one were to take your clear-cut Immanentism as final and
complete, the noblest half of religious experience of tip-toe expectation, of
unfulfilled expectation...would have no place.[11]

Despite his growing apprehension about Tyrrell's subjectivism, with
its resultant relativities and uncertainties, it was not until after Tyrrell's
death that von Hügel's newer convictions began to emerge. It was in his
post-1911 period that he began to assert with increasing forcefulness the
value of the institutional Church, the objective "givenness" of God, and
His unchanging created orders and truth patterns. Although von Hügel's
recoil from Tyrrell's immanentism was slow, it was undoubtedly certain.[12]
He became convinced he said, of "the intolerable insufficience of all
mere Immanence."[13] In 1918, he capped his opposition to Tyrrell's
immanental philosophy when he said:

I have come to see, more clearly than I used to do, how much of serious
unsatisfactoriness and danger there was especially in many of the philosophical
(strongly subjectivist) theories really held which *Pascendi* lumped together.[14]

Third, there is the profound difference between von Hügel's
personality and Tyrrell's which was to give birth to the wider issue as to
how the Modernists should advance their case in the Church. Von Hügel
was devout in a traditional sense, meticulous about ecclesiastical protocol, a strategist and planner, the master-mind behind the Modernist
movement. Tyrrell was by nature a skeptical mystic, easily exasperated
by the restraints of orthodoxy and the demands of protocol, volatile, and
temperamental. He despaired over von Hügel's scrupulosity and, at
times, resented his assumed role as overseer of the Modernist movement.
To von Hügel, Modernism was a cause; to Tyrrell, it was a conflict which
treatened to cut the nerve of his whole religious life. Von Hügel's piety
and devotion were unaffected either by his scholarship or by the acrid
debate over Modernism. For Tyrrell, however, religious life as a whole
seemed to be suspended on the outcome of the controversies in which he
was involved. In von Hügel's decisions there was always a cautious
restraint; in Tyrrell's there was usually a reckless abandon.

It was these differences which explain some critical remarks which
Tyrrell made about von Hügel. Miss Petre, for example, quoted Tyrrell as
asking: "Is this man, who has been to me as my own conscience, a
coward?"[15] Again, to Robert Dell, Tyrrell enlarged on this theme:

I had to insist lately that he [von Hügel] must, for his credit, sign *some* article or
other expressing his views. He had given me a hundred mystical reasons for not sign-
ing this or that or the other article. I said they were all excellent reasons; but people
would reasonably ask how the man, who argued the *Rinnovamento* people to face
excommunication and the destruction of their work, was not willing to face the like
himself.[16]

In April, 1906, Tyrrell wrote of his disapproval to von Hügel charging that
he should have acted differently in the Modernist crisis, given his strong
beliefs.[17]

This brief analysis of the role played by Tyrrell and von Hügel in the Modernist struggle offers some help in seeing why Tyrrell was condemned while von Hügel was not, but there are still large enigmas which surround this episode. The future of suspected Modernists was apparently decided on the basis of three crucial issues: the extent of their deviation from orthodox theology, the nature of their commitment as churchmen to the Roman Catholic Church, and the extent of their influence in the Church. On the first issue, it would seem clear that even if von Hügel was not quite as culpable as Tyrrell in his heterodoxy, he was certainly still less than orthodox. This fact, however, was mitigated in the eyes of the authorities by his orthodox churchmanship and what was deemed by comparison, to be his minimal influence as a layman. Whereas Blondel and von Hügel yielded to the pressures of orthodoxy, Tyrrell openly repudiated the directives of the authorities, believing that he could not offer allegiance to the spirit of the "Antichrist." It is significant to note, too, that little of von Hügel's writing was published before the Pope's condemnation of Modernism in 1907. His *Mystical Element* appeared in 1908, *Eternal Life* in 1912, the first series of *Essays and Addresses* in 1921, and *The Reality of God* in 1931. Presumably, Church authorities assumed that von Hügel's influence was negligible in the Church since he had not attempted to disseminate his views in book form. By contrast, Tyrrell's literary production was extensive, his attacks on orthodoxy bold and searing, his theology skeptical and radical.

The question as to why Tyrrell was rejected by the Church, while some of his friends were allowed to continue within it, is therefore complex. At least it seems clear that the problem of condemnation was both broader and narrower than the question of heterodoxy. It was broader because it also incorporated the issues of churchmanship, status, and influence; it was narrower because the intrusion of these other issues mitigated or exacerbated the doctrinal issues which were at stake.

Despite appearance, then, the papal condemnation was aimed at Modernism considered as a movement rather than at its theology considered in abstraction from the movement. Undoubtedly the former included the latter, but the latter did not necesssarily imply all of the former. For there is clear evidence that the authorities feared that Modernism was a clandestine, subversive movement which was organizing itself on all sides with the intent of destroying the Church. The vastly exaggerated estimates made by Tyrrell and other Modernists of the secret following they had in the Church probably only fueled these fires and brought on the clumsy emasculation that took place. If von Hügel's involvement in organizing the movement was not well known to the authorities — and it may not have been — then presumably their failure to condemn him might have meant that a latitude of thought which traversed the bounds of orthodoxy and was informed by the Modernist spirit could be tolerated (albeit with pain and disapproval), provided it was counter-balanced by prudent submission to the authorities and careful participation in theological discussion.

In view of this procedure, we have a clue about how some of Tyrrell's heresy of yesterday could become the Church's orthodoxy of today. If a relationship does exist between Modernism and the New Catholicism, there are only a limited number of ways in which the connection can be explained. First, it could be argued that contemporary Catholicism has capitulated to the old Modernist heresy. But few Roman Catholics will find this a very attractive solution. Second, it could be argued that the Modernists were prophets before their time. Vatican II and its subsequent developments have shown that the concerns of the Modernists were quite legitimate. But this solution has its problems as well. If the first option condemns the contemporary Church for its heresy, the second condemns the Church at the turn of the century for repudiating Modernism. There is very little indication that Roman Catholics wish to do this. Indeed, those like Küng and Schillebeeckx who would be the most sympathetic to Modernist views are also the most insistent that Modernism was wrong and that its condemnation was entirely legitimate.[18]

If Roman Catholics are to retain their convictions, first, that Modernism was justifiably condemned and, second, that Vatican II and post-Vatican II theology are not heretical, then a *via media* has to be found between the two options considered so far. This explanation must be constructed out of a series of qualifications about condemnation of Modernism. The distinction between Modernism as a movement and Modernism as a theology will have to be developed. If such a distinction can be made, then it will follow that much of the condemnation which fell on Tyrrell can be explained, not so much by his ideas as by his actions. Furthermore, the diversity of the Modernist movement will have to be underlined. When this is done, it will be seen that even when the Modernist's ideas were being condemned, it was more of an abstract system that was struck down rather than a position to which all Modernists agreed.

In certain respects, Tyrrell could complain quite justifiably that the Pope had constructed a straw man in his encyclical *Pascendi*. The post-1906 changes in his thought placed him almost within the bounds of orthodoxy in some crucial matters. Thus by distinguishing between thought and action in Tyrrell and between Tyrrell's thought and the condemned Modernist system, it becomes possible to see that certain of his ideas have actually escaped authentic censure. Furthermore, some ideas which were legitimate were alloyed to others that were clearly wrong. His contention, for example, that collegiality should be endorsed by the Church was entirely correct, as the Council showed, but the chief corollary Tyrrell drew from this belief, that the Pope was the Antichrist, is obviously wrong. Thus by refining even further the core of ideas placed outside of the Church's censure, it becomes possible to see how some of his views have finally triumphed in the Church with the magisterium's approbation. Granted the connection between Tyrrell's Modernism and the Council's *aggiornamento*, a Roman Catholic has no real option but to seek a *via media* along these lines.

But is the connection between Tyrrell and the New Catholicism established beyond reasonable doubt? If it is not, then the need for explanations falls away. This offers itself as an alluring way out of the impasse. Whether it needs to be taken depends on whether or not the parallels between Tyrrell's views and those of the New Catholicism can be explained away.

Parallels, however, exist in at least three distinct areas. The first concerns the relation between the natural and the supernatural. Tyrrell's philosophy was built around the idea of Divine immanence. Because God is "in" man, the Transcendent is "in" the historical; the supernatural is native to man's being. It never impinges on his consciousness as something essentially alien to his self-experience. The Divine is as natural to man's inner life as the sunshine is to his outer life. The Divine is not only in man but also in the processes of nature. Both man and nature communicate the reality of God.

The presence of God in the soul of every man was not explicitly affirmed by the Council. What was stated was that a sense of mystery pervades human existence and that the Logos has illuminated every man. But it is significant to note that the idea of sacramentality which was so much to the fore in Tyrrell's thought has reappeared in the New Catholicism. Its presence in the Council documents may be explained by a new concern with mystery and a matching concern to repudiate a legal concept of the Church and of faith. Consequently, it cannot be disputed that this emphasis is implicitly affirmed.

The presence of God "in" the world led Tyrrell to seek a reconciliation between Roman particularism and religious universality. He attempted to hold the two together, and in this attempt the Council paralleled his thought. Neither Tyrrell nor the Council was willing to argue that all religions are equally true, yet neither wished to say that Rome alone possessed all Christian truth. What both did say was that Rome had the most truth, but this statement did not mean that others had none. Separation from Rome only meant separation from truth in its fullness.

The second matter in which interesting echoes of Tyrrell are to be heard in the New Catholicism concerns revelation. In the final stage in his thinking, Tyrrell attempted to hold a Liberal view of revelation as experience together with the traditional notion that revelation is to be identified with the biblical text. Thus he hoped to combine an element of stability, which Liberalism lacked, with one of personal immediacy, which conservative thought lacked. Vatican II did likewise.

Arising out of this conception of revelation, paradoxical as it may be, Tyrrell argued that every believer has access to the *depositum fidei*. This contact he identified with the Spirit's life within. The presence of the Spirit, in turn, gave the laity a new importance and made collegiality an indispensable part of his theology. The Council repeated these ideas, first by introducing a decree on the laity, which was the first of its kind in conciliar history, and then, second, by endorsing collegiality.

The third area where parallels are to be found concerns the nature of the Church. Tyrrell argued consistently that the Modernist debate was predominately over what kind of Church Roman Catholics wanted. Did they want one formed on the motif of the People of God, such as was belatedly endorsed at Vatican II, or did they want one structured by the traditional and legalistic hierarchy? To be sure, Vatican II did not allow the issue to be posed in this form. It is not a question of either/or, the Council said, but of both/and. Yet the fact that the *Populus Dei* motif appeared at all is a remarkable echo of Tyrrell's contention.

In attempting to relate today's *aggiornamento* to yesterday's Modernism, there appear to be only two real options. The first is to seek a *via media* between saying that Modernism was wholly heretical and that the New Catholicism is wholly orthodox. The second is to deny any kind of theological relationship between the two movements. The second option would appear to be an infinitely more difficult route to take than the first.

Once the connection is acknowledged and a *via media* is sought, then it follows that the prophetic significance of Tyrrell's ideas must be recognized. The Council itself taught that the Church's historians must lay aside the polemical concerns when dealing with matters of the past. Past disputes must "be presented from an ecumenical point of view, so that at every point they may more accurately correspond with the facts of the case."[19] Nowhere could this injunction be followed with greater profit than in the condemnation of George Tyrrell; no single aspect of Church history demands to be reassessed more than that of Catholic Modernism. Indeed, the future of the New Catholicism no less than the effect it will have on the theology of the future depend on a satisfactory account of the new changes in Catholic thought relative to historic Modernism. If the New Catholicism cannot dissociate itself sufficiently from Modernism, or if it cannot dissociate some of the Modernists' ideas from the Pope's condemnation, a suspicion will develop that it, too, is a "synthesis of all heresies." Yet if it dissociate itself from its precursor too vigorously, a similar suspicion will develop. The new theologians it will be felt, are either unacquainted with what the Modernists really thought or they are familiar with that theology but do not care to relate it to what they think. The New Catholicism cannot dissociate itself from Modernism too strongly, nor can it go on pretending that Modernism is nothing more than a closed chapter in Church history.[20] However it chooses to deal with the issue, the pioneering work of George Tyrrell must be recognized. Someone may then like to recall that Tyrrell foresaw the day when his views would be accepted; it was merely his timing that was off.

NOTES TO THE INTRODUCTION

[1]Pope Pius X in his encyclical *Pascendi* said of the Modernists: "lacking the solid safeguards of philosophy and theology, nay more, thoroughly imbued with the poisonous doctrines taught by the enemies of the Church, and lost to all sense of modesty, [they] put themselves forward as reformers of the Church; and, forming more boldly into line of attack, assail all that is most sacred in the work of Christ, not sparing even the Person of the Divine Redeemer...there is no part of Catholic truth which they leave untouched, none that they do not strive to corrupt." *Encyclical Letter ("Pascendi Gregis") of our most Holy Lord Pius X. by Divine Providence Pope on the Doctrines of the Modernists*, Official trans. (London: Burns and Oates, 1907), pp. 4-5

[2]*Pascendi* itself suggested the idea of a clandestine organization, and this suggestion was repeated in September, 1910 in the *Sacrorum Antistitum*.

[3]See, for example, R. Garrigou-Lagrange, "La Nouvelle Théologie où va-t-elle?" *Angelicum*, 23 (1946): 126-45. Cf. Léonce de Grandmaison, "Une Nouvelle Crise Moderniste est-elle possible?" *Etudes* 76 (1923): 641-43. Vatican II similarly raised fears of a new and resurgent Modernism. In England, a counter-movement known as Unitas came into being "to combat and refute the neo-modernism which is eating at the very vitals of the Church and destroying the faith of the people of our country." Some scholars predicted an open rupture in the Church. See Pierre Debray, *Schisme dans l'église* (Paris: Editions de la Table Ronde, 1965). Cf. Alexander Dru, "Modernism and the Present Position of the Church," *Downside Review* 86, 271 (April 1965): 177-80; John Ratté, "The Specter of Modernism," *Commonweal* 82, 17 (23 July 1965): 530-33.

[4]Emille Poulat produced the bio-bibliographical index to Loisy's works in the biography written by A. Houtin and F. Sartiaux entitled *Alfred Loisy, sa vie, son oevre* (Paris: Editions du Centre National de la Recherche Scientifique, 1960).

[5]Up to 1929, the basic bibliography for Modernism is Jean Rivière's *Le modernisme dans L'église: Etude d'histoire religieuse contemporaire* (Paris: Librairie Letouzey et Ané, 1929). In 1940, Rivière updated his work in "La Crise Moderniste devant l'opinioin d'aujourd'hui," *Revue des sciences religieuses* 20, 1 (Jan.-April 1940): 140-82. For the recent period see Roger Aubert, "Recent Literature in the Modernist Movement," *Concilium*, vol.

17: *Historical Investigations*, ed. Roger Aubert (New York: Herder & Herder, 1966), pp. 91-108.

[6]See, for example, René Marlé, *Au coeur de la crise moderniste, le dossier d'une controverse inédite* (Paris: Editions Montaigne, 1960); Maurice Blondel-Auguste Valensin, *Correspondence (1899-1912)*, 2 vols., (Paris: Aubier, 1957); Maurice Blondel, Lucien Laberthonnière, *Correspondence philosophique*, ed. C. Tresmontant (Paris: Editions du Sevil, 1961); A. Louis-David, ed., *Lettres de George Tyrrell à Henri Bremond* (Paris: Aubier-Montaigne, 1971).

[7]See, for example, Emille Poulat, *Histoire, dogme et critique dans la crise moderniste* (Paris: Casterman, 1962); Lucio da Veiga Coutinho, *Tradition et histoire dans la controverse moderniste 1898-1910* (Rome: Typis Pontificae Universitatis Gregorianae, 1954); Jean Madiran, *L'Intégrisme, histoire d'une histoire* (Paris: Nouvelles Editions Latines, 1964); Francois Rodé, *Le miracle dans la controverse moderniste* (Paris: Beauchesne et Ses Fils, 1965). These represent some of the more important recent studies which are germane to the broader question of Modernism, but omitted here is the flourishing literature on the Italian expression of it.

[8]Alec Vidler, *A Variety of Catholic Modernists* (Cambridge: Cambridge University Press, 1970); Lawrence F. Barmann, *Baron Friedrich von Hügel and the Modernist Crisis in England* (Cambridge: Cambridge University Press, 1972); John J. Heaney, *The Modernist Crisis: von Hügel* (Washington: Corpus Books, 1968); Joseph P. Whelan, *The Spirituality of Friedrich von Hügel* (Westminster: The Newman Press, 1972).

[9]T. Loome, "A Bibliography of the Published Writings of George Tyrrell (1861-1900), *Heythrop Journal* 10, 3 (July 1969): 280-314; "A Bibliography of the Printed Works of George Tyrrell: Supplement," *Heythrop Journal* 11, 2 (April 1970): 161-69.

[10]M.D. Petre, ed., *George Tyrrell's Letters* (London: T. Fisher Unwin, 1920). The second collection is Anne Louis-David's, cited earlier. In addition, there have been other publications of letters, such as from the Raffalovich correspondence, but though they are of interest personally they have not thrown much new light on Tyrrell's theology. See Thomas Loome, "Tyrrell's Letters to Andre Raffalovich," *The Month* 1 (Feb. 1970): 95-101; Meriol Trevor replied in *The Month*, 1 (April 1970): 199.

[11]John Ratté, *Three Modernists: Alfred Loisy, George Tyrrell, W.L. Sullivan* (London: Shed and Ward, 1968), pp. 143-256.

[12]Meriol Trevor, *Prophets and Guardians: Renewal and Tradition in the Church* (London: Hollis and Carter, 1969), pp. 32-41.

[13]A. Loisy, *George Tyrrell et Henry Bremond* (Paris: Emile Nourry, 1936).

[14]M.D. Petre, *Life of George Tyrrell, 1884-1909*, vol. 2: *Autobiography and Life of George Tyrrell* (London: Edward Arnold, 1912); M.D. Petre, *Von Hügel and Tyrrell: The Story of a Friendship* (London: J.M. Dent and Sons

Ltd., 1937). The collection of Tyrrell letters edited and selected by Miss Petre is cited above. Further information on Tyrrell is included in Petre's autobiography, *My Way of Faith* (London: E.M. Dent and Sons, 1937). Her articles on Tyrrell are useful as far as they go. See "The Creative Elements of Tyrrell's Religious Thought," *Modern Churchman* 28, 12 (March 1929): 695-703; "George Tyrrell and Friedrich von Hügel in their Relation to Catholic Modernism," *Modern Churchman* 17, 3 (June 1927): 143-54; "New Wine in Old Bottles," *Modern Churchman* 22, 4 (July 1932): 212-18; "A Religious Movement of the First Years of our Century," *Horizon: A Review of Literature and Art* 6, 35 (Nov. 1942): 328-42; "Still at It: The Impasse of Modern Christology," *Hibbert Journal* 20, 3 (April 1922): 401-10. See also M.D. Petre, *Modernism: Its Failures and Its Fruits* (London: T.C. and E.C. Jack, 1918).

NOTES TO CHAPTER ONE

[1]The first official response to Modernist ideas was issued by Leo XIII in January, 1899, and entitled *Testem benevolentiae*; in this letter the Church was warned against Americanism. In September of that year, Leo turned his attention to France. *Depuis le jour* warns against irresponsible attitudes in biblical scholarship. The task of heading off the Modernist challenge, however, fell to Leo's successor Pius X. He issued three sharp condemnations. The Italian Modernists were rebuked in July, 1906, in *Pieni l'animo*. *Lamentabili* was the second condemnation, and *Pascendi* the third. For bibliography relating to these documents, see R. Aubert, *Le problème de l'acte de foi; données traditionelles et résultats des controverses récentes* (Louvain: E. Warny, 1945), pp. 380-87. Cf. Léonce de Grandmaison, "Pie X., Pope," *Etudes* 117 (1908): 291-307; Henri Holstein, "Au temps du modernisme," *Etudes* 291 (1956): 212-33.

[2]Friedrich von Hügel, *Selected Letters*, ed. Bernard Holland (London: J.M. Dent, 1928), p. 248.

[3]Basil Willey, *Nineteenth Century Studies: Coleridge to Matthew Arnold* (London: Clarke, Irwin and Co., 1949), p.9.

[4]George Tyrrell, Letter to *Guardian*, No. 3233 (20 Nov. 1970): 1896-97.

[5]For a succinct summary of Tyrrell's debate with the Vatican see Barmann, *Baron Friedrich von Hügel and the Modernist Crisis in England*, pp. 204-6.

[6]B.M.G. Reardon, "The Prelude to the Contemporary Crisis in Roman Catholicism," *The Expository Times*, 79, 7 (April 1968): 202. See also his essay "Newman and the Catholic Modernist Movement," *The Church Quarterly* 4 (July 1971): 50-60. Derek Holmes, however, has argued that Newman was far closer to Modernism than Reardon allows, and E. Kelly, who further substantiates this claim, notes that this philosophical proximity to Modernism should not have been left unexplored by those at the Second Vatican Council for whom Newman was a guiding light. Derek J. Holmes, "Newman and Modernism," *Baptist Quarterly* 24 (July 1972): 335-41; E. Kelly, "Newman, Wilfrid Ward, and the Modernist Crisis," *Thought* 48 (Winter 1973): 508-19.

[7]Charles E. Osborne, "George Tyrrell: A friend's impressions," *Hibbert Journal* 8, 2 (Jan. 1910): 256.

[8]Henry Bettenson, *Documents of the Christian Church* (London: Oxford University Press, 1963), p.384.

[9]Tyrrell to Raffalovich, 1901. Bl. Lib.

[10]Loisy thus stated that Modernism represented "the desire to adapt Catholic faith to the intellectual, moral and social needs of the present time." Alfred Loisy, *Simples réflexions sur le décret du saint-office Lamentabili sane exitu et sur l'encyclique Pascendi dominici gregis* (Ceffonds: Chez L'auteur, 1909), p.15. Similarly, von Hügel's theology has been described as an unconscious search "for a synthesis of all the factors of life, a unity whose richness will consist in the wealth of diversities it contains." Michael de la Bedoyere, *The Life of Baron von Hügel* (London: J.M. Dent and Sons, 1951), p.69.

[11]Rivière, *Le modernisme dans l'Eglise*, p.12

[12]A.L. Lilley, *Modernism: A Record and Review* (London: Sir Isaac Pitman and Sons, 1908), pp. 258-60.

[13]Percy Gardner, "Modernism and Modernity," *Modern Churchman* 1, 1 (April 1911): 17.

[14]Petre, *Modernism* p. 114.

[15]Paul Sabatier, *Modernism*, trans. C.A. Miles (London: Adelphi Terrace, 1908), p. 65.

[16]Alec Vidler, *The Modernist Movement in the Roman Church: Its Origins and Outcome* (Cambridge: Cambridge University Press, 1934), p. 183.

[17]F.O.S. Schiller, "Infallibility and Toleration," *Hibbert Journal* 7 (Oct. 1908 — July 1909): 76.

[18]Raymond Dulac, "Les devours du journaliste Catholique selon le Bienheureux Piex," *La pensée Catholique* 23 (1952): 68-87.

[19]There are documents indicating that Pius X was both callous and brutal in his handling of the Modernists, that subsequently he allowed the new zealots for orthodoxy, the so-called integrists, to terrorize the Church, that he had in effect resuscitated the Inquisition, and that he had

utilized the *Sodalitium Pianum* as secret police. The result was that innocent people were persecuted and the Church was unnecessarily divided.
See Carlo Falconi, *The Popes in the Twentieth Century: From Pius X to
John XXIII*, trans. Muriel Grindrod (Boston: Little, Brown and Co., 1967),
pp. 42-69.

[20]Martin Clark, "The Theology of Catholic Modernism," *The Church
Quarterly Review* (Oct.—Dec. 1963): 458-70.

[21]Petre, "New Wine in Old Bottles," p. 214.

[22]Tyrrell, *M*, p. 106.

[23]J. Lebreton, *The Encyclical and Modernist Theology*, trans. Alban
Goodier (London: Catholic Truth Society, 1908), p. 73.

[24]Edwin Aubrey, "What is Modernism?" *Journal of Religion*, 25 (Oct.
1935): 428.

[25]George Tyrrell, "Medievalism and Modernism," *Harvard Theological
Review* 1 (April 1908): 304-5.

[26]*Dec. UR*, 10.

NOTES TO CHAPTER TWO

[1]Trevor, *Prophets and Guardians*, p. 44. Cf: R. Jenkins, "Tyrrell's
Dublin Days," *The Month* 42 (July—August 1969): 8-15. See also D.
Macpherson, "Von Hügel on George Tyrrell," *The Month* 4 (December
1971): 178-80.

[2]Tyrrell, *A&L I*, pp. 92-148.

[3]*Ibid.*, pp. 172-232. See also A. Thomas, "George Tyrrell: From Student
Days," *Heythrop Journal* 11 (April 1970): 170-72.

[4]Petre, *A&L II*, pp. 40-47. Cf. Tyrrell, *A&L I*, pp. 264-78.

[5]Petre, *A&L II*, pp. 131-145.

[6]George Tyrrell, "A Perverted Devotion," *The Weekly Register*, C, No.
2608 (16 Dec. 1899): 797-800.

[7][George Tyrrell], "The Anglo-Roman Pastoral," *Pilot* 3, no. 53 (2
March 1901): 282; [George Tyrrell], "Lord Halifax Demurs," *The Weekly
Register* 103, no. 2680 (3 May 1901): 549-50; Halifax [George Tyrrell], "The
Recent Anglo-Roman Pastoral," *The Nineteenth Century and After* 49
(May 1901): 736-54.

[8]Petre, *A&L II*, pp. 167-75.

[9]Tyrrell to Colley, 10 August 1901. Archives, Eng. Prov. S.J.

[10]Gabriel Daly, "Some Reflections on the Character of George
Tyrrell," *Heythrop Journal* 10 (July 1969): 261.

[11]Percy Gardner accepted Tyrrell's tentative explanation of his difficulties, saying that "it is evident that we cannot expect to find in his works any logical or consistent scheme of belief...he never really absorbed the Roman position." Percy Gardner, *Modernism in the English Church* (London: Methuen and Co., 1926), p. 51. There is striking evidence to the contrary, however, in the early sermons which Tyrrell preached, some of which are still preserved in their manuscript form in the Archives of the English Provincial Society of Jesus at Farm Street, London. These sermons, written out in full, give a forceful and lucid defense of many traditional Catholic beliefs. There is no reason to think that Tyrrell was not entirely sincere in proclaiming these truths as he did. Arnold Lunn was probably correct in complaining, then, that "Tyrrell's self-portrait is coloured by the mood of later years. He has read into his boyish memories the disillusionment of middle age." Arnold Lunn, *Roman Converts* (London: Chapman and Hall, 1924), p. 135.

[12]Wilfrid Ward, *Last Lectures* (London: Longmans, Green and Co., 1918), pp. 207-8.

[13]Petre, *A&L II*, pp. 249-55.

[14]*Ibid.*, pp. 503-6.

[15]Bedoyere, *Life of Baron von Hügel*, p. 198.

[16]George Tyrrell, Letter to *Times* (30 September 1907), p. 5.

[17]George Tyrrell, Letter to *Times* (1 October 1907), p. 4.

[18]*Ibid.*

[19]Petre, *von Hügel and Tyrrell*, pp. 161-62.

[20]von Hügel, *Selected Letters*, 23 April 1909, p. 141.

[21]Tyrrell to Raffalovich, Bl. Lib.

[22]Tyrrell's death was carefully documented by Petre. See entries for the period 6 July 1909 to 3 August 1909, in her personal diary, *Petre Papers*, British Museum, MSS 52374. A full account of the problems connected with his death and burial is also provided in *Petre Papers*, British Museum, 52638, from which her published summary in *A&L II*, pp. 420-46, is drawn. See also Alfred Loisy, *Mémoires pour servir à l'histoire religieuse de notre temps*, 3 vols. (Paris: Emile Nourry, 1930-31), 3:143.

[23]Maisie Ward, *Insurrection and Resurrection*, vol. 2: *The Wilfrid Wards and the Transition* (London: Sheed and Ward, 1937), p. 186.

[24]Tyrrell, *M*, p. 155.

[25]*Ibid.*, p. 157.

[26]Cited by Petre, *A&L II*, p. 285.

[27]Tyrrell, "Revelation as Experience," *Petre Papers*, Br. Mus. MSS 52369.

NOTES TO CHAPTER THREE

[1]Percy Gardner, *Anglican Liberalism* (London: Williams and Norgate, 1908), p. 137.

[2]Friedrich Schleiermacher, *A Critical Essay on the Gospel of St. Luke*, trans. Canon Thirlwall (London: J. Taylor, 1825), p. ix, n.

[3]Tyrrell to von Hügel, November 1906, *von Hügel and Tyrrell Correspondence*, Br. Mus. Add. MSS. 44929.

[4]Tyrrell, *OW*, p. 56.

[5]See Edgar Hocedez, *Histoire de la théologie au XIX siècle*, 3 vols. (Bruxelles: L'Edition Universelle, 1947), 3:13-319.

[6]Cf. Pittenger's complaint that classical theism "has consistently stressed God's independence, absoluteness and aseity, to the neglect of his relatedness to the world; one might say that a good deal of theism, in this mode, has been closer to a metaphysic of divine indifference than to one of love." Norman Pittenger, "Process Theology Revisited," *Theology Today* 27, 2 (July 1970): 212.

[7]Tyrrell, *LO*, p. 25.

[8]Tyrrell, *LC*, p. 7.

[9]Cf. Tyrrell, *CCR*, pp. 223-44. Throughout human history, "man's soul has uniformly breathed the air of a supernatural atmosphere." (Tyrrell, *LO*, p. xxix).

[10]Tyrrell, "Revelation as Experience: A Reply to Hakluyt Egerton," *Petre Papers*, Br. Mus. MSS 52369. This lecture was subsequently published by Thomas Loome, "Revelation as experience: An Unpublished Lecture of George Tyrrell," *Heythrop Journal* 12 (April 1971): 117-49.

[11]Tyrrell defined a Modernist as one who believed in the possibility of a "synthesis between the essentials of Christianity and the assured results of criticism" (Tyrrell, *CCR*, p. xv). At the end of his life, he was still insisting that by *synthesis* he did not mean "a compromise involving the sacrifice of anything vital or essential to either side" (Tyrrell, "Medievalism and Modernism," pp. 304-5).

[12]Tyrrell, *T&C*, p. 91; Tyrrell, *HS*, p. 31; Tyrrell, *FM I*, p. 234. The Kantian elements in Tyrrell's thought proved to be most disturbing to Catholic orthodoxy. Indeed, Pius X in his encyclical *Pascendi* drew attention to these ideas and repudiated them. See also Joseph Bampton, *Modernism and Modern Thought* (London: Sands and Co., 1913), pp. 36-37; cf. André Marc, *Raison philosophique et religion révélée* (Paris, Desclée de Brouwer, 1955), pp. 14-27.

[13]Tyrrell, *LO*, p. 68.

[14]Blondel, Tyrrell declared, "reaches by a methodical research what I stumble on by luck, or, at least, by instinct." Cited by Petre, *A&L II*, p. 92.

[15]For Blondel's conception of action see James Somerville, *Total Commitment: Blondel's L'Action.* (Washington: Corpus Books, 1968);

Augustin Valensin, "Maurice Blondel: A Study of His Achievement," *Dublin Review* 224 (First Quarter 1950): 94; Katherine Gilbert, *Maurice Blondel's Philosophy of Action* (Chapel Hill: University of North Carolina Press, 1924), p. 47; Henri Bouillard, "The Thought of Maurice Blondel: A Synoptic Vision," *International Philosophical Quarterly* 3, 3 (Sept. 1964): 394.

[16]Louis Dupré, "Blondel's Religious Philosophy," *The New Scholasticism*, 40, 1 (Jan. 1966): 5.

[17]Cf. Schubert Ogden's chapter entitled "The Strange Witness of Unbelief," in *The Reality of God and Other Essays* (New York: Harper and Row; 1966), pp. 120-43.

[18]Tyrrell, *T&C*, pp. 20-21.

[19]*Ibid.*, p. 44.

[20]George Tyrrell, "The Making of Religion," *Month* 92 (Sept. 1898): 362. Cf. Tyrrell, *T&C*, p. 24.

[21]On the use of this expression in Tertullian, who was its originator, see Johannes Quasten, *Patrology*, 3 vols. (Westminister: The Newman Press, 1950), 2:266.

[22]Tyrrell to von Hügel, 3 January 1902, *Von Hügel and Tyrrell Correspondence*, Br. Mus. Add. MSS 44928.

[23]Tyrrell, *LO*, p. xvii.

[24]Tyrrell to Raffalovich, 7 Nov. 1900. Bl. Lib.

[25]Cite by Petre, *A&L II*, p. 414.

[26]George Tyrrell, "The Relation of Theology to Devotion," *Month* 94 (Nov. 1899): 461-73. Reprinted in Tyrrell's *FM I* as "The Relation of Theology to Devotion," pp. 228-52 and in Tyrrell's *T&C* as "Lex Orandi, Lex Credendi," pp. 85-105. Translated into French as "Théologie et Religion," *Annales de philosophie chrétienne* 41 (March 1900): 625-41.

[27]This statement needs qualification. It is an accurate description of his stance between January, 1904 and December, 1906. In the final year of his theological life, however, he moved back to a more conservative position.

[28]See Tyrrell's important chapter entitled "Mysteries a Necessity of Life," *T&C*, pp. 155-190; "The True and False Mysticism" in three chapters, in *FM I*, pp. 273-334.

[29]Tyrrell, *CCR*, p. 215.

[30]Panentheism is a term associated with the process theology derived from Whitehead and Hartshorne. These philosophers have sought to balance the Aristotelian notion of God as absolute, immutable, and infinite Being with the suggestion that part of Divine reality may in fact be relative, finite, and susceptible to the changes which created reality undergoes. Thus, in this view, God "is created as well as creative and is as much dependent upon the world, in fact, as the world is dependent upon him." Nels Ferré, "God Without Theism," *Theology Today* 22 (Oct. 1965): 375.

[31]See Hastings Rashdall, *Ideas and Ideals* (Freeport, N.Y.: Books for Libraries Press, 1968), pp. 138-39.

[32]Tyrrell, *CCR*, p. 29.

[33]Tyrrell, *LO*, pp. 207-08.

[34]Tyrrell said that between these two orders of reality "there exists a certain analogy whose precise nature is hidden just because we cannot compare its terms as we can those of thought and extension." (Tyrrell, *LO*, p. 58). See also Tyrrell, *HS*, pp. 314, 398; Tyrrell, *ER*, p. 6; Tyrrell, *FM I*, pp. 94-96, 144-46; Tyrrell, *OW*, pp. 4, 54, 74, 80, 228, 30; Tyrrell, *T&C*, pp. 39, 96, 232-31, 326-34; Julius I. Bella, "Father Tyrrell's Dogmas," *Church History* 7, 4 (Dec. 1939): 316-41.

[35]Belfield has suggested that Tyrrell's notion of analogy is a "unique form of the analogy of attribution...through the method of immanence to a universalized *via supereminentiae*." John H. Belfield, "The 'Theological' Method of George Tyrrell: A Study of the Modernist Crisis in the Light of George Tyrrell's Thought" (Ph.D. dissertation, The Catholic University of America, 1966), p. 195.

[36]To this "discrimination between substance and envelope we have been forced by the advance of human thought; by the progressive delimitation between the territories of subjective and objective, between vision and fact." Tyrrell, *CCR*, p. 145. See also Tyrrell, *ER*, pp. 24-25; Tyrrell, *T&C*, p. 90.

[37]Tyrrell, *LO*, p. 96; see also pp. 84-85.

[38]Tyrrell, *CF*, p. 81. See also Tyrrell, *LC*, pp. 180-81; Tyrrell, *FM I*, p. 234.

[39]Tyrrell, *LC*, p. 17. It was this conviction which led him to say, "how false and thin a conception of Christ he would have who, without distinguishing the spirit from the embodiment, should take the religion of the Synoptics or even of St. John or St. Paul as the sole and only legitimate expression of Christianity to be slavishly imitated by all future ages, to be a fetter on all progress and lawful variation." (Tyrrell, *LC*, p. 52). On this attempt to negotiate between the literal and metaphorical see J. Goetz, "Coleridge, Newman and Tyrrell: A Note," *Heythrop Journal* 14 (Oct. 1973): 431-36.

[40]Tyrrell, *CCR*, p. 184.

[41]Tyrrell to von Hügel, 12 November 1900, *Von Hügel and Tyrrell Correspondence*, Br. Mus. Add. MSS. 44927.

[42]Tyrrell, *LC*, p. 23. It is of interest to note that in 1894 or 1895 Tyrrell gave an eloquent defense of the traditional doctrine of bodily resurrection. "There are self-styled Christians," he said, "for whom this essential and almost central tenet of Christianity is a stumbling block on account of such shallow and puerile difficulties as I have alluded to ... They tell us that... the only resurrection to be insisted on is the moral resurrection from vice to virtue..." Tyrrell refused to accept this, arguing that "the resurrection of Christ's wounded body" was the genuine Catholic

doctrine. (The sermon is undated. The original manuscript is located in the Archives, Eng. Prov. S.J.).

[43]Tyrrell, *CCR*, p. 137 See F.M. O'Connor, "Tyrrell's Cross Roads," *Heythrop Journal* 5 (1964): 188-91.

[44]Tyrrell, *CCR*, p. 82. Richard Ballard has rightly pointed out that Tyrrell's employment of the genre of apocalyptic with its accent on the Transcendent clearly set him apart from the conventions of Liberal Protestantism. They looked for a consistent improvement of the world; Tyrrell dispaired of this happening and saw bodily resurrection as its refutation. The question still remains, however, whether the idea of resurrection was retained for its own intrinsic verity or whether it was simply the necessary vehicle for expressing the Transcendent. Seemingly different statements can be adduced from Tyrrell on this question which attest to a measure of fluidity in his thought. See Richard Ballard, "George Tyrrell and the Apocalyptic Vision of Christ," *Theology* 78 (Sept. 1975): 459-67; on the broader question of faith and the material world, see J. Root, "English Catholic Modernism and Science: The Case of George Tyrrell," *Heythrop Journal* 18 (July 1977): 271-88.

[45]Tyrrell to von Hügel, 13 July 1907, *Von Hügel and Tyrrell Correspondence*, Br. Mus. Add. MSS 44930.

[46]Tyrrell to von Hügel, 7 Feb. 1907, *Von Hügel and Tyrrell Correspondence*, Br. Mus. Add. MSS 52370.

[47]Tyrrell, *T&C*, p. 207.

[48]Tyrrell, *MAL*, p. 56. See Lewis May, *Father Tyrrell and the Modernist Movement* (London: Eyre and Spottiswoode, 1932), p. 176. In 1952, Carl Jung published his study on Job in which he argued that the Assumption of Mary should be seen as an expression of the Church's collective self-consciousness. Man wants to see a heavenly bride alongside a heavenly bridegroom, together symbolizing eternal comfort and security. This aproach, the Church replied, undermines the objective reality of which her doctrine is the expression. The same might also be said of Tyrrell's notion.

[49]Tyrrell, *LO*, p. 150.

[50]*Ibid.*, p. 68.

[51]Tyrrell, *FM I*, p. 266.

[52]*Con. LG.*, 1.

[53]*Ibid.*, 3.

[54]*Ibid.*, 48.

[55]*Ibid.*, 1.

[56]*Ibid.*, 9.

[57]*Ibid.*, 9, 10, 11, 21, 27.

[58]*Con. DV*, 2.

[59]*Con. SC*, 102, 106, 107, 109.

[60]*Ibid.*, 60-63, 79; *Con. LG*, 29.

[61]The Council did not apply the notion of sacramentality to nature; this is the major difference between its theology and that of Tyrrell at this point. The other differences are only those of emphasis and language.

[62]The point was made in John's opening speech at the Council in which he allowed that there is a distinction between "substance of the ancient doctrine of the deposit of faith" and "the way in which it is presented" (Walter Abbott, The Documents of Vatican II (London: Geoffrey Chapman, 1967), p. 715). The distinction was understood as more than that of language. John's statement precipitated a furor. See Antoine Wenger, Vatican II: Première session (Paris: Editions du Centurion, 1963), pp. 46-50.

[63]Edward Schillebeeckx, God the Future of Man (New York: Sheed and Ward, 1968); Gregory Baum, Man Becoming: God in Secular Experience (New York: Herder and Herder, 1970).

[64]Con. GS, 39.

[65]Barnabas Ahern, "The Eschatological Dimensions of the Church," in Vatican II: An Interfaith Appraisal, ed. John Miller (Notre Dame: University of Notre Dame Press, 1966), p. 299.

[66]Decln. NA, 2.

[67]Con. GS, 22.

[68]Con. LG, 14.

[69]Con. LG, 15.

[70]Ibid., 16. See also Yves Congar, "The People of God," in Vatican II: An Interfaith Appraisal, pp. 197-207.

[71]Karl Rahner, "The Teaching of the Second Vatican Council on Atheism," Concilium, vol. 23: The Pastoral Approach to Atheism, ed. Karl Rahner (New York: Paulist Press, 1967), pp. 7-24.

[72]Christopher Butler, The Theology of Vatican II (London: Darton, Longman and Todd, 1967), p. 167.

[73]Ibid., p. 126. Cf. Jean Daniélou, The Salvation of the Nations, trans. Angeline Bouchard (Notre Dame: University of Notre Dame Press, 1962).

[74]George Tyrrell, "Beati Excommunicati," Petre Papers, Br. Mus. MSS 52369.

[75]Pascendi, p. 17.

NOTES TO CHAPTER FOUR

[1]The Church, Tyrrell believed, was exercising a harmful effect on human life. In a letter to Bishop Mathew he said, "the Vatican cesspool remains to poison the religion and civilization of Europe.... The axe of legislation must be set to the roots of the tree." (The letter is dated simply 19 October. Archives, Eng. Prov. S.J.). On October 1, 1907, Tyrrell told Mathew that he was "pre-occupied in pulling down rather than in building up Churches." (Archives, Eng. Prov. S.J.). Later, on April 7, 1909, after the publication of *Pascendi*, Tyrrell said to von Hügel, "if Babylon is incurable the 'modernising' effort is the surest and solidest way to destroy her, and to save as many as possible from the wreck before the ship founders." (*Von Hügel and Tyrrell Correspondence*, Br. Mus. Add. MSS. 44931). It should be noted, however, that the letters in the Provincial Archives of the Society of Jesus are copies, unlike the rest of the correspondence in the British Museum.

[2]Tyrrell, *MAL*, p. 56.

[3]The letter is dated 30 September 1900, Archives, Eng. Prov. S.J.

[4]Petre, *A&L II*, p. 265.

[5]The letter is dated 31 December 1907, Archives, Eng. Prov. S.J.

[6]The letter is simply dated 15 December, Archives, Eng. Prov. S.J.

[7]Tyrrell, *CCR*, pp. 12-3. Tyrrell argued for decentralization and a measure of national autonomy in a letter to the Provincial, dated 17 November 1900: "to deal with those best minds [in England], needs a sympathy, a wealth, a subtlety, which the coarse-minded dogmatism of foreign theologians could not tolerate for a moment, and it is they eventually who rule us and prescribe for countries of whose condition they are as ignorant as they are of Christian charity and truthfulness" (Archives, Eng. Prov. S.J.). The Second Vatican Council later came to recognize the validity of the complaint. Seminary training should be geared to the conditions in which the priests will serve (*Dec. IM*, 1); worship should be in the vernacular (*Con. SC*, 37-40) and may vary from locality to locality (*Dec. UR*, 21, 23, 41, 42). There may even be variation in theological expression from nation to nation (*Dec. UR*, 4).

[8]The letter is simply dated 15 December (Archives, Eng. Prov. S.J.). Tyrrell, it is of interest to note, rejected the traditional notion of apostolic succession. This was a juridical notion, whereas the genuine succession was spiritual. Only the Christlike, he said, "are genuine successors of the Apostles" (Tyrrell, *EF*, p. 116). Only Christ knows who is in the real Church and only He is empowered to authenticate a man's ministry, be he bishop or priest.

⁹Tyrrell, *A&L II*, p. 413.

¹⁰Tyrrell, *CF*, p. 19. Prior to his Modernist phase, Tyrrell defended the notions of ecclesiastical and papal infallibility as strongly as he was later to deny them. In a sermon preached in 1899, Tyrrell defended Rome's claim to be in exclusive possession of the truth. "This note of exclusiveness and what is called 'intolerance' must mark the Church which Christ left on earth to continue his work. Does it mark any section of Christendom except the Church of Rome? Notoriously not... All indeed profess to be right, but only one professes to be infallibly right—Rome... If Christ does not speak to us in Rome when does he speak? To whom shall we go?" (Archives, Eng. Prov. S.J).

¹¹The letter is dated 3 January 1902, *Von Hügel and Tyrrell Correspondence*, Br. Mus. Add. MSS. 44928. Six years later Tyrrell could claim that the "hard and fast mechanical view of Scriptural inerrancy has yielded forever to a much looser, more flexible and dynamic notion of inspiration.... The inerrancy of General Councils must inevitably and *a fortiori* be re-interpreted with a similar latitude" (Tyrrell, *M*, p. 79).

¹²Tyrrell, *CF*, p. 20.

¹³Alfred Loisy, *L'Evangile et l'église,* 2d ed. (Bellevue: Chez l'auteur, 1903), p. 70.

¹⁴Tyrrell, *CF*, p. 61.

¹⁵*Ibid.,* p. 55.

¹⁶*Ibid.,* p. 53. The traditional explanation for this *transitus* has usually been worked out along the lines of development. See, for example, Owen Chadwick, *From Bossuet to Newman: The Idea of Doctrinal Development* (Cambridge: Cambridge University Press, 1957). Tyrrell endorsed the idea of development for some years but then moved beyond it. He charged that the Church had only applied the idea in a half-hearted fashion, stopping the process of development in the Middle Ages. But Tyrrell also maintained, especially towards the end of his life, that Scripture should provide the formal structure for religious belief. He then shuttled between these two positions as circumstance required. His most explicit statement on revelation is contained in his paper, "Revelation as Experience," *Petre Papers*, Br. Mus. MSS 52369.

¹⁷George Tyrrell, "L'Affair Loisy," *The Pilot* (2 Jan. 1904): 11.

¹⁸Tyrrell, "Medievalism and Modernism," p. 305.

¹⁹The letter is dated 25 January 1905, *Von Hügel and Tyrrell Correspondence*, Br. Mus. Add. MSS. 44929.

²⁰The letter is dated 27 January. Archives, Eng. Prov. S.J.

²¹This letter, written to A.L. Lilley and dated 4 October, 1907, has been deposited in the library of St. Andrews University, Scotland.

²²The letter is dated 29 June 1904, *Von Hügel and Tyrrell Correspondence*, Br. Mus. Add. MSS. 44928.

²³"Pius X," Tyrrell said in a typical remark, "is in the same case as a mad father, who orders his children to burn down the house...the vision

of Pius X is an incoherent and ugly as that of a nightmare" (Cited by Petre, *A&L II*, p. 405).

[24]The letter is dated 20 November 1904, *Von Hügel and Tyrrell Correspondence*, Br. Mus. Add. MSS. 44928.

[25]On the issue raised by the pastoral, see J. Holmes, "Some Notes on Liberal Catholicism and Catholic Modernism," *Irish Theological Quarterly*, 38 (Oct. 1971): 384-57; William Schoenl, "George Tyrrell and the English Liberal Catholic Crisis, 1900-01," *Downside Review* 92 (July 1974): 171-83.

[26][George Tyrrell], "Lord Halifax Demurs," *The Weekly Register* 103, No. 2680 (3 May 1901): 550.

[27]*Ibid.*

[28]The letter is dated 20 Feb. 1901, *Von Hügel and Tyrrell Correspondence*, Br. Mus. Add. MSS 44927. Three years later Tyrrell was still smarting from this pastoral and expressing indignation over it. In a letter to A.L. Lilley he explained the cause of his grief: "Now the Jesuit theologians hold that even *fallible* ecclesiastical rulings bind to *internal* assent under pain of mortal sin against faith though not of the particular mortal sin called 'heresy.' Also they hold that the Church's *indirect* teaching authority extends...to *all* natural truth... This is tantamount to an indirect jurisdiction over the whole field of human knowledge, as claimed in the Joint-Pastoral of 1901." (The letter is dated 30 January 1904, St. And. Lib.).

[29]Tyrrell, "Lord Halifax Demurs," p. 550.

[30]Writing under a pseudonym, Tyrrell explained that it "is in the collective mind of the Church, not in the separate mind of the Pontiff that the truth is elaborated...the Pope cannot be conceived to speak ex *cathedra* except when he professedly investigates the ecumenical mind (S.T.L. [George Tyrrell], Letter to *Weekly Register* 103, no. 2685 (24 May 1901), pp. 662-63).

[31]Cuthbert Butler, *The Vatican Council*, 2 vols. (London: Longmans and Green 1930), 2:95.

[32]*Ibid.*, pp. 144-45. Küng has argued that "it can be shown from the Acts of the Council how the Pope, when making binding statements of doctrine, must not act separately from the Church but only as representing the whole Church, with whom he must remain in contact. The Pope cannot by any means define arbitrarily or against the will of the Church as a whole; the Pope himself has to be on his guard against schism (Hans Küng, *The Living Church: Reflections on the Second Vatican Council*, trans. C. Hastings and M.D. Smith [London: Sheed and Ward, 1963], pp. 301-2). In view of the Council's rejection of St. Antonius's formulation which embodies Küng's view, it would be interesting to know which acts of the Council he had in mind when he made this statement.

[33]The letter is dated 30 September 1904, *Von Hügel and Tyrrell Correspondence*, Br. Mus. Add. MSS 449928.

[34]George Tyrrell, "Beati Excommunicati," *Petre Papers*, Br. Mus. MSS 52369. This paper, completed on 18 May, 1905, re-examined the nature of excommunication and it indicates that Tyrrell had counted the cost carefully before embarking on his campaign against Pius. Ironically, the paper was completed exactly twenty-six years after Tyrrell entered the Church on 18 May, 1879. The paper was later published as "L'Excommunication Salutaire," *Grande Revue* 44 (10 Oct. 1907): 661-72.

[35]*Dec. Ur*, 2.

[36]*Con. LG*, 22.

[37]*Ibid.*, 18, 20.

[38]*Ibid.*, 22.

[39]The episcopal college, it would appear, has two principles of unification: sacramental union with Christ and juridical relationship to the Pope (*Con. LG*, 27). From these two principles arise different conceptions of infallibility. In certain circumstances, some papal actions are infallible. But there is also an additional infallibility which the college possesses, not through relationship with the Pope but through union with Christ (*Con. LG*, 25). Infallibility, the Council stated, was a consequence of revelation and there is only one *Dei verbum* which is in the possession of all the People (*Con. LG*, 25, 49). The College's sacramental infallibility, therefore, seems to be a particular application of a more general infallibility characterizing all Christian People and arising out of the collective *sensus fidei*. Theoretically, this triumvirate of infallibilities in People, College and Pope should always act in concert but the possibility is at least present of infallible disagreements. The Pope could seek to enforce infallible teaching on the Church which it could with equal infallibility resist. See Klaus Morsdorf, "Decree on the Bishops: Pastoral Office in the Church," *Commentary on the Documents of Vatican II*, 5 vols., trans. William Glenn-Doepel *et al.* (London: Burns and Oates, 1966-67), 2:165-300.

[40]Cornelius Williams, "The Church is Hierarchical," *Vatican II: The Church Constitution*, ed. Austin Flannery (Dublin: Sceptre Books, 1966), p. 86.

[41]*Con LG Addenda*, 3.

[42]See Edward Schillebeeckx, *Vatican II: The Real Achievement*, trans. H.J.J. Vaughan (London: Sheed and Ward, 1967), pp. 16-17.

[43]*Con LG. Addenda*, 3.

[44]*Con LG*, 22.

[45]Butler, *Theology of Vatican II*, 105.

[46]See E. Schillebeeckx, "Un nouveau type de laic," *La nouvelle image de l'église*, ed. Bernard Lambert (Paris: Editions Maine, 1967), 177.

[47]Cf. Hans Küng, "The Charismatic Structure of the Church," *Concilium*, IV, No. 1 (April, 1965), 23-33.

[48]*Con. LG*, 10.

[49]Butler, *Theology of Vatican II*, 110.

[50]*Pascendi....*, 33.

[51]*Ibid.*, 47.

[52]See C. Mehok, "Hans Küng and George Tyrrell on the Church," *Homiletic and Pastoral Review*, 72 (Jan., 1972), 57-66.

NOTES TO CHAPTER FIVE

[1]See Paul Minear's analysis "A Protestant View" in Miller, ed., *Vatican II: An Interfaith Appraisal*, pp. 66-88.

[2]H.J. Schroeder, ed., *Canons and Decrees of the Council of Trent* (London: B. Herder Book Co., 1960), p. 17.

[3]*The Encyclical Letter of Pius IX, 8th December, 1864, Proclaiming the Jubilee of 1865; with the Syllabus of LXXX. Errors which He Condemns* (Edinburgh: George McGibbon, n.d.), p. 5.

[4]*Con. De Rev.*, cap. 11.

[5]*Con. De Fide*, cap. 4.

[6]*The Great Encyclical Letters of Pope Leo XIII* (New York: Benziger Brothers, 1903), p. 272.

[7]*Ibid.*, p. 298.

[8]*Pascendi*, pp. 44-45.

[9]*Con. DV*, 11.

[10]René Latourelle, *Theology of Revelation* (Cork: Mercier Press, 1968), pp. 453-83.

[11]Butler, *Theology of Vatican II*, p. 56.

[12]George H. Tavard, *The Dogmatic Constitution on Divine Revelation of Vatican Council II, Promulgated by Pope VI, November 18, 1965: Commentary and translation* (London: Darton, Longman and Todd, 1966), p. 167.

[13]*Con. DV*, 1.

[14]*Ibid.*, 7.

[15]Butler, *Theology of Vatican II*, p. 34. Tavard has also argued that in "its personal dimension, revelation is inseparable from the act of hearing and of responding by which man acknowledges in his heart and in public that God spoke in the past and that he speaks here and now." (Tavard, *The Dogmatic Constitution*, p. 24).

[16]*Pascendi*, p. 9.

[17]This analysis is partly at variance with the one offered by Francis O'Connor in his two articles entitled "George Tyrrell and Dogma—I," *Downside Review* 85, 278 (Jan. 1967): 16-34, and "George Tyrrell and Dogma—II," *Downside Review*, 85, 279 (April 1967): 160-82. These differences should be noted: (1) O'Connor has discerned three phases in the progressive period of Tyrrell's thought. These run from August, 1900 to January, 1904; January, 1904, to the end of 1906; 1907 to the time of Tyrrell's death. The additional phase arises out of the belief that the second "Semper Eadem" article was really different from the first one published in January, 1904, and not, as Tyrrell claimed, a clarification of what had been said previously. This is a matter of judgment but it seems wiser to accept Tyrrell's word. (See Petre, *A&L II*, p. 211). (2) O'Connor has

overlooked Tyrrell's important article "Ecclesiastical Development" in the pre-1900 period and cited the article on Sabatier as his first reflection on this theme. (3) The point of transition from conservative to progressive O'Connor dates at August, 1900, with the publication of "The Mind of the Church." This is an extraordinary judgment in view of Tyrrell's own testimony regarding "The Relation of Theology to Devotion" which came out in November, 1899. (See Tyrrell, *T&C*, pp. 85-86; Petre, *A&L II*, p. 98).

[18]See Tyrrell's essay entitled "Ecclesiastical Development," *Month* 90 (Oct. 1897): 380-90.

[19]Tyrrell, *FM I*, p. 124.

[20]*Ibid.*, p. 133.

[21]*Ibid.*, p. 131.

[22]*Ibid.*, p. 127.

[23]Tyrrell, "Ecclesiastical Development," p. 383.

[24]Tyrrell, *FM I*, p. 143.

[25]*Ibid.*

[26]*Ibid.*, p. 150.

[27]Rivière, *Le modernisme dans l'église*, pp. 196-97.

[28]Petre, "Still at it: The Impasse of Modern Christology," p. 402.

[29]Tyrrell, *FM I*, p. 199.

[30]*Ibid.*, p. 163.

[31]Tyrrell, *CF*, p. 140.

[32]Tyrrell, *LO*, pp. 207-15.

[33]Tyrrell, *FM I*, p. 192.

[34]Tyrrell, *CF*, p. 21.

[35]Tyrrell to A.L. Lilley, 15 January 1904, St. And. Lib. In another letter to A.L. Lilley he said: "I ventured in the January *Month* to set Wilfrid Wardism and School-theology in sharp opposition as hopelessly irreconcilable. What I really mean is that the latter is a lost cause, but the reactionaries, like the Babylonian dragon, have swallowed my cake of pitch and fat and hair. I really feared I had exaggerated the grotesque impossibility of their position, but the letters of congratulation that pour in assure me that I have not done so at all." The letter is dated 4 January 1904, St. And. Lib.

[36]Tyrrell, *T&C*, p. 4.

[37]*Ibid.*

[38]*Ibid.*, p. 295.

[39]*Ibid.*

[40]*Ibid.*, pp. 353-54.

[41]See Tyrrell's lecture entitled "Revelation as Experience: A Reply to Hakluyt Egerton," *Petre Papers*, Br. Mus. MSS 52369.

[42]*Ibid.*

[43]Tyrrell, *CCR*, p. 95.

[44]*Ibid.*, p. 94.

⁴⁵Tyrrell, "Revelation as Experience."

⁴⁶*Con. DV*, 9.

⁴⁷The final phrase of the Council's statement cited above which states that Scripture and tradition are to be accepted and venerated "with the same sense of devotion and reverence" is lifted from the Council of Trent's declaration ("pari pietatis affectu ac reverentia"). Standing by itself, however, this phrase does not demand that Scripture and tradition be separated as Trent suggested. On the contrary, equal reverence is given to both, not because of their independence but because of their coinherence in the same source of revelation. On the debate over the interpretation of Trent see Gabriel Moran, *Scripture and Tradition: A Survey of the Controversy* (New York: Herder and Herder, 1963), pp. 89-98; Guiseppe Alberigo, "The Council of Trent: New Views on the Occasion of its Fourth Centenary," *Concilium*, vol. 7: *Historical Problems of Church Renewal*, ed. Rogert Aubert and Anton Weiler (New York: Paulist Press, 1965), pp. 38-48.

⁴⁸*Con. DV*, 10.

⁴⁹*Con. LG*, 12.

⁵⁰Tyrrell, *M*, p. 53.

⁵¹*Ibid.*, p. 55

⁵²*Ibid.*, p. 53.

⁵³*Pascendi*, p. 39.

⁵⁴*Ibid.*, p. 31.

NOTES TO CHAPTER SIX

¹Vidler, *A Variety of Catholic Modernists*, p. 111.

²Thomas Michael Loome, "The Enigma of Baron Friedrich von Hügel—as Modernist—I," *Downside Review* 91, 302 (Jan. 1973): 16-25. In this and succeeding essays, Loome carefully evaluates the role of von Hügel in Modernism and charges that the picture Barmann presents tells us less about the Baron than it does about Barmann's presuppositions. See "The Enigma of Baron Friedrich von Hügel—as Modernist—II," *Downside Review*, 91, 303 (April 1973): 123-40; "The Enigma of Baron Friedrich von Hügel—as Modernist—III," *Downside Review* 91, 304 (July 1973): 204-30. Whether Loome is correct or not, it is indisputable that at the time of Tyrrell's condemnation the Baron boldly advanced Modernist ideas and orchestrated the movement. On this subject, see also Ronald Burke, "An Orthodox Modernist with a Modern View of Truth," *Journal of Religion* 57, 2 (April 1977): 123-43.

³Vidler, *A Variety of Catholic Modernists*, p. 110.

[4]Friedrich von Hügel and Charles Briggs, *The Papal Commission and the Pentateuch* (London: Longmans, Green and Co., 1906).

[5]Friedrich von Hügel, "Experience and Transcendence," *Dublin Review* 138 (April 1906): 357.

[6]Richard Emrich, *The Conception of the Church in the Writings and Life of the German-English Philosopher Baron Friedrich von Hügel* (München: Ernst Reinhardt Verlag, 1939), p. 47.

[7]von Hügel, *Essays and Addresses on the Philosophy of Religion*, 2 vols. (New York: Dutton, 1933), 1:233.

[8]Emrich, *Conception of the Church*, p. 46.

[9]Friedrich von Hügel, *Selected Letters*, p. 141.

[10]Cited by Petre, *Von Hügel and Tyrrell*, p. 59; see also von Hügel, *Selected Letters*, p. 75.

[11]*Ibid.*, p. 139.

[12]See Maude Petre, "Von Hügel and the Great Quest," *Modern Churchman* 21 (Dec. 1912): 479.

[13]von Hügel, *Essays*, 1:36.

[14]von Hügel, *Selected Letters*, pp. 248-49.

[15]Petre, *Von Hügel and Tyrrell*, p. 146.

[16]*Ibid.*, p. 147.

[17]*Ibid.*, pp. 175-84.

[18]Schillebeeckx has suggested that not everyone who bore the Modernist stigma was necessarily a Modernist, but this qualification does not affect the contention that for him, no less than for Küng, Modernism was wrong. See Schillebeeckx, *Vatican II: A Struggle of Minds*, p. 30.

[19]*Dec. Ur*, 10.

[20]In this connection it is worth noting the statement by F.O.S. Schiller, written in 1909:

> It is quite conceivable that in due course, when the more cautious sympathisers with modern thought have risen by dint of years to the higher posts in the hierarchy...some successor of Pius X will be moved to issue another Encyclical which, after splitting a vast number of hairs to prove that what is now sanctioned is not identical with what was condemned before, will define the sense in which a Modernist attitude may be permitted and concede the substance of what has lately been denied" ("Infallibility and Toleration," p. 87).

See also Lawrence Barmann, "The Heresy of Orthodoxy," *Theology* 71, 580 (October 1968): 456-62.

A SELECTED BIBLIOGRAPHY OF GENERAL WORKS

Aubert, Roger. *La théologie catholique au milieu du xxe siècle*. Paris: Casterman, 1954.

Baraúna, Guilherme and Congar, Yves (eds.) *L'église de vatican II: études autour de la constitution conciliaire sur l'église*. 3 vols. Paris: Les editions du cerf, 1966.

Barmann, Lawrence F. *Baron Friedrich von Hügel and the Modernist Crisis in England*. Cambridge: University Press, 1972.

Barth, Karl. *Ad Limina Apostolorum: An Appraisal of Vatican II*. Translated by Keith R. Crim. Richmond: John Knox Press, 1968.

Basset, Bernard. *The English Jesuits: From Campion to Martindale*. London: Burns and Oates, 1967.

Bedoyere, Michael de la. *The Life of Baron von Hügel*. London: J.M. Dent and Sons Ltd., 1951.

Berkouwer, G.C. *Recent Developments in Roman Catholic Thought*. Translated by J.J. Lamberts. Grand Rapids: Eerdmans, 1961.

_____.*The Second Vatican Council and the New Catholicism*. Translated by L.B. Smedes. Grand Rapids: Eerdmans, 1965.

Blondel, Maurice. *Letter on Apologetics and History and Dogma*. Translated and introduced by Alexander Dru and Illtyd Trethowan. London: Harvill Press, 1964.

Burtchaell, James T. *Catholic Theories of Inspiration Since 1910*. Cambridge: The University Press, 1969.

Butler, Christopher. *The Theology of Vatican II*. London: Barton, Longman and Todd Ltd., 1967.

Catholic Directory. London: Burnes and Oates, 1887-1910.

Chadwick, Owen. *From Bossuet to Newman: The Idea of Doctrinal Development*. Cambridge: Cambridge University Press, 1957.

Cock, Albert A. *A Critical Examination of von Hügel's Philosophy of Religion*. London: Hugh Rees, 1953.

Congar, Y.M.J. and Peuchmaurd, M., eds. *L'église dans le monde de ce temps: constitution pastorale 'gaudium et spes'*. 3 vols. Paris: Les éditions du cerf, 1967.

Coutinho, Lucio Da Veiga. *Tradition et histoire dans la controverse moderniste 1898-1910*. Romae: Typis Pontificae Universitatis Gregorianae, 1954.

Cullman, Oscar. *Vatican II: The New Direction*. Selected and arranged by James D. Hester. New York and Evanston: Harper and Row, 1968.

Dakin, Hazard A. *Von Hügel and the Supernatural*. London: Society for Promoting Christian Knowledge, 1934.

Delmont. *Modernisme et modernistes: en Italie, en Allemagne, en Angleterre, et en France*. Paris: P. Lethielleux, 1909.

Dimnet, E. *La pensée catholique dans l'Angleterre contemporaine*. Paris: Librairie Victor Lecoffre, 1906.

Elliot-Binns, L.E. *English Thought, 1860-1900: The Theological Aspect*. London: Longmans, Green and Co., 1956.

Emrich, Richard S. *The Conception of the Church in the Writing and Life of the German-English Philosopher Baron Friedrich Von Hügel*. München: Ernst Reinhardt Verlag, 1939.

Encyclical Letter (Pascendi Gregis) of our Most Holy Lord Pius X. by Divine Providence Pope, on the Doctrines of the Modernists. Official translation. London: Burns and Oates Ltd., 1907.

Falconi, Carlo. *The Popes in the Twentieth Century: from Pius X to John XXIII*. Translated by Muriel Grindrod. London: Wiedenfeld and Nicholson, 1967.

Fawkes, Alfred. *Studies in Modernism*. London: Smith, Elder and Co. Ltd., 1913.

Gardner, Percy. *Modernism in the English Church*. London: Methuen and Co. Ltd., 1926.

Gilbert, Katherine. *Maurice Blondel's Philosophy of Action*. Chapel Hill: University of North Carolina, 1924.

Hales, E.E.Y. *The Catholic Church in the Modern World: A Survey from the French Revolution to the Present*. Garden City, NY: Image Books, 1960.

Heaney, John J. *The Modernist Crisis: Von Hügel*. Washington and Cleveland: Corpus Books, 1968.

Henry, A.M., ed. *Les relations de l'église avec les religions non Chrétiennes*. Paris: Les éditions du cerf, 1966.

Hocedez, Edgar. *Histoire de la théologie au xixe siècle*. 3 vols. Bruxelles: L'édition universelle, 1947.

Houtin, Albert and Sartiaux, Felix. *Alfred Loisy: sa vie, son oeuvre*. Edited by Emille Poulat. Paris: Editions du centre national de la recherche scientifique, 1960.

Küng, Hans. *The Council and Reunion*. Translated by Cecily Hastings. London: Sheed and Ward, 1962.

_____. *The Living Church: Reflections on the Second Vatican Council*. Translated by Cecily Hastings and N.D. Smith. London: Sheed and Ward, 1963.

Lambert, Bernard, ed. *La nouvelle image de l'église*. Paris: Editions Maine, 1967.

Lebreton, J. *The Encyclical and Modernist Theology.* Translated by Alban Goodier. London: Catholic Truth Society, 1908.

Lemius, J.B. *Catechism on Modernism according to the Encyclical 'Pascendi Dominici Gregis' of His Holiness, Pius X.* Translated by John Fitzpatrick. London: R. and T. Washbourne Ltd., 1908.

Lester-Garland, L.V. *The Religious Philosophy of Baron von Hügel.* London: J.M. Dent and Sons Ltd., 1932.

Lewis, Leicester Crosby. *The Philosophical Principles of French Modernism.* Philadelphia: University of Pennsylvania, 1925.

Lilley, A.L. *Modernism: A Record and Review.* London: Sir Isaac Pitman and Sons Ltd., 1908.

Loisy, Alfred Firmin. *L'évangile et l'église.* 2 ed. rev. Bellevue: Chez l'auteur, 1903.

Madiran, Jean. *L'intégrisme: histoire d'une histoire.* Paris: Nouvelles éditions latines, 1964.

Major, H.D.A. *English Modernism: It's Origin, Methods, Aims.* Cambridge, MA: Harvard University Press, 1927.

Marlé, René. *Au coeur de la crise moderniste: le dossier d'une controverse inédite.* Paris: Editions Montaigne, 1960.

May, Lewis J. *Father Tyrrell and the Modernist Movement.* London: Eyre and *Spottiswoode*, 1932.

McNamara, Kevin, ed. *Vatican II: The Constitution on the Church.* London: Geoffrey Chapman, 1968.

Mercier, Désiré. *Modernism.* Translated by Marian Lindsay. London: Burns and Oates, 1910.

Miller, John H., ed. *Vatican II: An Interfaith Apparisal.* Notre Dame and London: University of Notre Dame Press, 1966.

Moss, C.B. *The Old Catholic Movement, Its Origins and History.* London: S.P.C.K., 1964.

Nédoncelle, Maurice. *La pensée religieuse de Friedrich von Hügel.* Paris: Libraire Philosophique J. Vrin, 1935.

Novak, Michael. *The Open Church: Vatican II, Act II.* New York: The Macmillan Co., 1964.

Nunn, H.P.V. *What is Modernism?* London: Society for Promoting Christian Knowledge, 1932.

O'Brien, Elmer, ed. *Theology in Transition: A Bibliographical Evaluation, 1954-64.* New York: Herder and Herder, 1965.

Paliard, Jacques and Archambault, Paul. *Etudes Blondéliennes.* Paris: Presses Universitaires de France, 1951.

Pawley, Bernard C., ed. *The Second Vatican Council: Studies by Eight Angelican Observers.* London, New York and Toronto: Oxford University Press, 1967.

Petre, M.D. *Life of George Tyrrell, 1884-1909.* Vol. II of *Autobiography and Life of George Tyrrell.* London: Edward Arnold, 1912.

_____. *Alfred Loisy: His Religious Significance.* Cambridge: Cambridge University Press, 1944.

_____. *Von Hügel and Tyrrell: The Story of a Friendship.* London: J.M. Dent and Sons Ltd., 1937.

Poulat, Emille. *Histoire, dogme et critique dans la crise moderniste.* Paris: Casterman, 1962.

Prévost, Robert. *Vatican II: Pierre ou le chaos?* Paris: Editions de la Table Ronde, 1965.

Purdy, W.A. *The Church on the Move: The Characters and Policies of Pius XII and John XXIII.* London: Hollis and Carter, 1965.

Quick, Oliver Chase. *Liberalism, Modernism and Tradition.* London: Longmans, Green and Co., 1922.

Ranchetti, Michele. *The Catholic Modernists: A Study of the Religious Reform Movement 1864-1907.* Translated by Isabel Quigley. London: Oxford University Press. 1969.

Ratté, John. *Three Modernists: Alfred Loisy, George Tyrrell, W.L. Sullivan.* London: Sheed and Ward, 1968.

Rivière, Jean. *Le modernisme dans l'église: étude d'histoire religieuse contemporaine.* Paris: Libraire Letouzey et Ane, 1929.

Rodé, François. *Le miracle dans la controverse moderniste.* Paris: Beauchesne et Ses Fils, 1965.

Roux, Hébert. *Détresse et promesse de vatican II: réflexions et expériences d'un observateur au concile.* Paris: Editions du Seuil, 1967.

Rynne, Xavier (pseud.) *Letters from Vatican City: Vatican II (First Session), Background and Debates.* London: Faber and Faber, 1963.

_____. *The Second Session: The Debates and Decrees of Vatican Council II, September 29 to December 4, 1963.* London: Faber and Faber, 1964.

_____. *The Third Session: The Debates and Decrees of Vatican Council II, September 11 to November 21, 1964.* London: Faber and Faber, 1965.

_____. *The Fourth Session: The Debates and Decrees of Vatican Council II, September 14 to December 8, 1965.* London: Faber and Faber, 1966.

Sabatier, Paul. *Modernism: The Jowett Lectures, 1908.* Translated by C.A. Miles. London: Adelphi Terrace, 1908.

Sacrosanctum Oecumenicum Concilium: Constitutiones, Decreta, Declarationes. Rome: Libreria Editrice Vaticana, 1966.

Schillebeeckx, E.H. *Vatican II: The Real Achievement.* Translated by H.J.J. Vaughan. London and Melbourne: Sheed and Ward, 1967.

_____. *Vatican II: A Struggle of Minds and Other Essays.* Translated by M.H. Gill. Dublin: Gill and Son, 1963.

Smith, Warren Sylvester. *The London Heretics, 1870-1914.* London: Constable and Co. Ltd., 1967.

Steinmann, Jean. *Friedrich von Hügel: Sa vie, son oeuvre et ses amitiés.*
Paris: Editions Montaigne, 1962.

Stewart, Herbert Leslie. *Modernism, Past and Present.* London: John
Murray, 1932.

Sutcliffe, Edmund F. *Bibliography of the English Province of the Society
of Jesus, 1773-1953.* London: The Manresa Press, 1957.

Trevor, Meriol. *Prophets and Guardians: Renewal and Tradition in the
Church.* London: Hollis and Carter, 1969.

Vidler, A.R. *The Modernist Movement in the Roman Church: Its Origins
and Outcome.* Cambridge: Cambridge University Press, 1934.

_____. *A Variety of Catholic Modernists.* Cambridge: The
University Press, 1970.

Vorgrimler, Herbert, ed. *Commentary on the Documents of Vatican II.*
Translated by William Glen-Doepel, Hilda Graef, Richard Strachen,
Ronald Walls and R.A. Wilson. 3 vols. London: Burns and Oates and
Herder and Herder, 1967.

Ward, Maise. *The Wilfrid Wards and the Transitions.* Vol. 2:
Insurrection and Resurrection. London: Sheed and Ward, 1937.

Wenger, Antoine. *Vatican II: première session.* Paris: Éditions du
Centurion, 1963.

What we Want: An Open Letter to Pius X. From a Group of Priests.
Translated by A.L. Lilley. London: John Murray, 1907.

Woodlock, Francis, S.J. *Modernism and the Christian Church.* London:
Longmans, Green and Co., 1925.